# HOW TO RAISE A STREET-SMART CHILD

# HOW TO RAISE A STREET-SMART CHILD

## THE PARENT'S COMPLETE GUIDE TO SAFETY ON THE STREET AND AT HOME

## GRACE HECHINGER

FAWCETT CREST • NEW YORK

A Fawcett Crest Book
Published by Ballantine Books
Copyright © 1984 by Grace Hechinger

Library of Congress Catalog Card Number: 83-1418

ISBN 0-449-20841-9

This edition published by arrangement with Facts On File Publications

Manufactured in the United States of America

First Ballantine Books Edition: September 1985

For Fred

# Contents

# Acknowledgments

My work on this book had the benefit of many people's knowledge, advice and encouragement. To name everyone would require a chapter of its own. I am grateful to all those who shared their experiences or their expertise. Many who are quoted directly also contributed valuable background information and insights.

Since so little published research is available on children as crime victims, I am indebted to those who offered me their knowledge and led me to the work of others: James Cartier of the Juvenile Justice Center in San Marcos, Texas; Ann Downer of the Committee for Children in Seattle; David Finkelhor, head of the Family Violence Research Program at the University of New Hampshire; Carole Garrison, assistant professor of Criminal Justice at the University of Akron; Martin Gipson, Department of Psychology, University of the Pacific; Roger Hart, associate professor of Environmental Psychology at the Graduate Center of City University; Faye Warren of the National Crime Prevention Council; and Nicholas Zill, president of Child Trends.

My special thanks go to representatives of the police who gave generously of both their time and thoughtful concern, chief among them: Jack Meeks and Charles Bonaventura of the New York City Police Department; James Humphrey and Nathaniel Topp of the Detroit Police Department; Thomas

Oates of the Montclair, New Jersey, Police Department; and Terry McGill and Teri Poppino of the Portland, Oregon, Police Bureau.

Others whose contributions were particularly helpful include: Ed Muir, head of safety for the United Federation of Teachers; Stanley Rideout, chief of security for the Pittsburgh Schools; Phil King of the National Education Association; Headmaster Robin Lester and PTA President Mary Linda Zonana of the Trinity School; Dr. Edward A. Davies, chief of pediatrics at Lenox Hill Hospital; Steven Levenkron, a psychologist affiliated with Montefiore Hospital; Karolynn Siegel, New York psychologist; Gretchen Lengel and Peggy Bradt of the Parents League of New York; Roberta de Plas of S.T.O.P.; Loreli Damron of the TOPS program in the Charlottesville-Albermarle County School District in Virginia; Tamar Hosansky and Pamela McDonnell of the Safety and Fitness Exchange, John Phelon of the Utah Department of Public Safety; and the Kiwanis International Foundation.

Invaluable support and encouragement came from friends and colleagues: Leonard Buder, Susan Butler, Janet Chan, Nancy Evans, Alan Kurzweil, Myra, Mel and Jacob Lipman, Kim and Manny Weintraub, and Seymour Wishman.

My sons, Paul and John, cheerfully endured their mother's preoccupation and, in addition, offered many pertinent suggestions.

Finally, I owe a special debt of another kind to my husband, Fred, for his patience, his editorial help, his enduring support, his humor, and, most of all, his love.

New York
June 1984

# ◼ Introduction ◼

"You can't be that worried about me when I'm out at night if you can go to sleep so early," my teenage son said a few years ago. I told him it's not that I didn't worry; of course I did. But I added that I felt I'd taught him as much as I could. The rest was up to him now—and a bit of luck. If I was able to sleep, it was because I knew I'd done my best to teach him how to protect himself.

Children growing up in today's world need to gain a sense of personal security and safety. There are so many assaults on our sense of security that we are sometimes tempted to believe being defensive and fearful is the right approach after all. With everything that could happen, shouldn't we keep ourselves always on guard? But we also have to think again of how terrible it would be to live with constant anxiety. Always living with fear is much worse than many of the minor traumas we may eventually have to face. And so, we want to give our children a sense of security in what is undeniably an insecure world.

Fortunately, our children do not have to hide at home to be secure. It is possible to live with an awareness of the crime and danger around us without becoming unduly fearful or paranoid. What we need to do is teach our children to take reasonable precautions. At times it may be difficult for us to be good role-models. We must modify some of our habits. We do not walk alone on deserted streets late at night, give rides to hitchhikers or let strangers into our homes. It is not only our children but all of us who have to live with these kinds of preventive measures.

My experiences with my own two boys have made me aware of the need to teach personal safety. While they were growing up, I wondered how effectively I had taught them. Sometimes I worried that I might have made them too careful or even fearful; at others I wondered if I had been concerned enough. Much of the advice given in this book covers what I wish I had known when my children were still small. My safety instructions were often hastily improvised. Luckily, most of them seemed to work.

Safety education is part of every parent's responsibility. The best protection you can give your children is to teach them how to recognize difficult situations, how to avoid them if possible and, if not, how to react in the safest manner.

Think of teaching about safety as you do about fire drills. In school children are trained, when a fire alarm sounds, to get in line and walk calmly out of the building. Fire drills are practiced regularly. There is no need to frighten children by telling them all the gory details of what might happen, such as burning or suffocating from smoke fumes. The point of matter-of-fact practice and instructions is that danger can be avoided. No one objects to fire drills on the grounds they might scare children. In all safety talks, we must always emphasize what children should do to protect themselves, never the bad things that might happen to them.

I have written *How to Raise a Street-Smart Child* as a concerned parent with a special knowledge of education, not as an expert in self-defense or crime prevention. In the course of my research, I have interviewed police officers, psychologists, psychiatrists, people involved in neighborhood safety programs, school safety officials, children and the parents of children who have been victims. I have also read a great deal about crime and personal safety and observed self-defense and safety classes for children.

Books about children's safety, when they exist at all, are frequently filled with horror stories, case histories as well as complicated instructions in physical self-defense, advice that can actually be dangerous. This book is different. It goes beyond the usual ''Don't Talk to Strangers'' line and offers down-to-earth information and practical suggestions for parents to protect their children's safety.

No specific physical defense techniques—holds, kicks, punches and the like—are described here because no one, child or adult, can learn these techniques from a book. Learning physical self-defense is like learning to drive a car or sail a boat: you must learn by doing. And you must be committed to practicing until you have mastered certain skills. Correct supervision and practice with a qualified instructor are also necessary. In addition, learning to judge when to use these techniques is as important as the specific measures themselves. When and how a child can be taught physical self-defense depends on the child's age and other factors.

Unfortunately, parents are often frustrated and confused when searching for ways to teach their children personal safety basics. Many tend to be shy about being specific, especially when discussing sexual molestation. Throughout this book I will stress how you can have simple, straightforward talks about these problems.

*How to Raise a Street-Smart Child* is arranged so that after you have read the first two chapters, you may either continue to the end or select the subjects most important to you. Chapter 3 deals with younger children (between five and eight) getting ready to go out on their own. Chapters 4 and 5 discuss mugging and street crime. Chapter 6 describes how you can help a child after a bad experience. Chapters 7 and 8 treat sexual abuse both from someone known to a child and from a stranger. Chapter 9 deals with school-related safety problems. Chapter 10, also for younger children, is about safety in traffic and cars. Chapter 11, for all ages, discusses a child's behavior at home, whether alone, with parents or baby-sitters. Chapter 12 offers suggestions about what to do if your child is missing and discusses whether or not to have the child fingerprinted.

Many grade school and high school students are reluctant to report unpleasant or alarming incidents to their parents. They are afraid of subsequent excessive restrictions on their activities, of being blamed for not having prevented the incident or of simply not being taken seriously.

I hope this book will help parents and children speak with each other more openly about safety and about ways of preventing trouble; both generations will benefit. We cannot make our children completely safe, but we can reduce the risks by

teaching them how to avoid potential dangers and by establishing good communication. In addition, we can minimize the
undesirable aftereffects if unpleasant incidents do happen, and
help youngsters to handle them more effectively.

While being realistic in protecting our children, we also want
them to grow and thrive in the knowledge that the world is not
primarily a threatening place. Yes, there are some people—
young and old—who might want to harm them and about whom
they need to be warned, but the majority of strangers are harmless and even friendly. Our goal is to teach our children, by our
attitudes and actions, that most adults can be trusted to care
about children's welfare and happiness—and yet that they must
be careful about the few who cannot.

# HOW TO RAISE A
# STREET-SMART CHILD

# ■ 1 ■

# Living in a
# Dangerous World

O<small>N</small> a fall afternoon when my older son, Paul, was nine, the phone rang. The mother of one of his friends was on the line asking with real concern whether Paul had come home safely. Yes, I replied, surprised at the question. I understood her anxiety when she explained that her son had just returned unharmed after he and another boy had been mugged at knifepoint. Paul had been with them until a few minutes before the incident. Even though he had been spared the scary experience, I was as upset as if he had been directly involved. It was such a near miss; it could happen to Paul or any other child at any time.

Such incidents of casual violence—and their aftermath—have become part of our lives. We acknowledge them grudgingly for ourselves and with even greater reluctance for our children, and we hope that like lightning they will not strike close to home. Yet each time we hear about an ugly episode, it diminishes our sense of personal safety. Whether we live in a bustling city or a placid suburb, we worry about the impact of crime and violence on our lives—and with good reason.

"We cut off the children's television," *New York Times* columnist Russell Baker has written with wit and poignance about every parent's dilemma, "because we feared all that violence would turn them into monsters. Soon they were reading the newspapers and at grips with the real world. . . . But what the real world offered was even worse." Baker's solution: cut off the children's newspapers and give each a television set. "They haven't been at grips with the real world for weeks, thank heaven for Kojak, Starsky and Hutch."

Many parents would like to turn off the real world in which their children are growing up. And many news events that contain horrors for people of all ages become even more frightening for families with children.

One ironic example of how the real adult world can be more frightening than children's traditional imaginary fears was the discovery of cyanide-laced Extra-Strength Tylenol® capsules in 1982 and how it heightened parents' concern about the possible poisoning of Halloween candy.

The deaths in the Chicago area from poisoned Tylenol about a month before Halloween with its tales of witches and goblins, caused many parents to carefully monitor their children's trick-or-treat activities. Everyone was disturbed by the Tylenol scares, but children and families were distressed the most by the knowledge of one more reason for fear and mistrust.

The idea of anyone poisoning children's Halloween candy should be unthinkable; yet in 1982 it became a real worry for parents, another problem to deal with. Here was a case where the real news proved to be more frightening and bizarre than any story created for television.

Some communities banned door-to-door trick-or-treating and offered alternatives such as hayrides, costume contests and parades. Others planned to hand out toys or money instead of candy. In some places, centers were set up where a child's bag of candy could be X-rayed, and some hospitals offered to X-ray holiday treats to make sure they did not contain hidden pins or razor blades.

A mother in Stillwater, Oklahoma, told a reporter she would accompany her two children on their rounds and inspect every piece of candy they were given. She also said she might even substitute candy she had bought for the candy her children received. Some of her neighbors, she said, had banned trick-or-treating, "but I just couldn't say no when the kids enjoy it so much. They see all the costumes in the stores and they know it's Halloween. I'm just going to be very careful." Many parents across the country followed suit in their own fashion.

Others accepted the example of Jane Byrne, then Chicago's mayor, who said simply, "I would not allow my children to take candy this particular Halloween." And a Massachusetts woman said, "With all the problems around, you can't be too careful about safety and children. I don't feel we're taking Halloween away from the youngsters. The children know what is going on." She reported that a little girl had said, "You're right. It's not worth a poisoned candy bar."

And for Atlanta families a few years ago, Russell Baker's suggestion to turn off real life would also have been welcome. For nearly two years in that city, there had been more than twenty killings and mutilations of school-age children.

During that tense time, there were some changes in the way Atlanta people lived. Curfews were imposed by the city for the evening hours, despite the fact that most abductions apparently occurred during the day. Schools began imposing tight security measures to protect students who might be alone in school buildings or playgrounds.

During the height of the scare, parents began routinely to

restrict their children's movements and to call the police immediately if children could not be found. The news media began campaigns urging children not to go anywhere without parental approval. In many black neighborhoods, where most of the victims had lived, people said they felt trapped, as though they were living in a state of seige.

The tension and fear were felt by the Atlanta children. There were reports that some cringed at the sight of an approaching stranger. Others thought it necessary to travel in groups armed with sticks. Many children experienced recurring nightmares. Even after a suspect was apprehended and eventually convicted and the murders stopped, anxiety lingered and community vigilance persisted.

In another well-known incident, the first day that six-year-old Etan Patz had been allowed to walk alone to the school bus stop in New York's Greenwich Village he disappeared. Despite thorough police searches and some false clues, he has not been seen since the May day he vanished in 1979. The bus stop is a block and a half from the Patz home. His mother had watched him for most of the way from a fire escape. "You have to let them start having a little independence," she said quietly as she went over the incident.

The family had considered the neighborhood safe. Other children had walked alone to the bus. In spite of all this, like most parents, they had cautioned Etan about not going anywhere with strangers. Mrs. Patz told a newspaper reporter that the boy "thinks everyone of all ages is wonderful, trustworthy and kind."

Some people believe that Etan was kidnapped by the North American Man-Boy Love Association, a homosexual organization that promotes the legitimacy of emotional and sexual love between adult men and young boys and argues that state laws making such relationships illegal should be repealed. The family still does not know what happened to Etan.

The Tylenol scare, the Atlanta killings and the newspaper and television stories that reported the disappearance of Etan Patz reflect every parent's worse fears. Fortunately, few children are victims of serious crimes or violence. But when such incidents occur and are reported by the media, the news spreads quickly over phones and in school hallways. Every time a child is victimized, it makes countless other parents and children afraid. When told she was going to visit Atlanta, a six-year-old girl said, "Oh, it's dangerous for children there. There are bad people there that kidnap and kill them."

Stories of danger to other children make us feel that it could always happen to us—no matter how remote the possibility. Any story of calamity will make parents just a bit anxious; much as we would like to, we cannot forget that we have to teach our children to cope with a dangerous world.

The news media deal with the spectacular aspects of crime, but the more mundane aspects have touched all our lives. The impact was brought home to me when we were buying our older son's first bicycle. His heart was set on a special model. As we looked at the different bikes, a salesman warned, "I wouldn't buy one of those for my kid. They are the first to be stolen."

As parents, we faced a familiar dilemma. Was it better to tell a nine-year-old to settle for a less desirable bike because potential thieves would consider it less desirable as well? Or should we give him his special favorite accompanied by a warning about the dangers that came with it? Neither alternative seemed very attractive.

We decided to take the prudent course and bought a more conservative bike—a choice that looked like the lesser of two evils. Did our son enjoy it less? Paul does not remember the incident now, but he does remember enjoying his first bike. I will never forget it. The pleasure of selecting a gift for our child was marred by the darker considerations of the streets.

Caution is a response of many parents to living in the modern world. We could have chosen to ignore the potential dangers. Perhaps Paul's bike would never have been stolen. But the odds in New York City were such that we believed prudence to be a better part of valor.

And the fact is that we fool ourselves if we think our children are not aware of street dangers. Children themselves know what they face whether or not they tell us they are afraid.

Fears of violence, crime and personal injury are common among children. More than two-thirds of the youngsters in a recent survey said yes when asked, ''Do you feel afraid that somebody bad might get into your house?'' A national study of more than 2,000 seven to eleven-year-olds, designed by Nicholas Zill, a psychologist and president of the non-profit research organization Child Trends, for the Foundation for Child Development, demonstrated that 68 percent were afraid an intruder might enter their homes. This fear was reported by all the children who participated in the study regardless of how old they were, whether they lived in urban or rural areas or whether they were poor or middle-class. Seventy-five percent of the girls and 62 percent of the boys expressed such fear.

This same group of children was asked, ''When you go outside, are you afraid someone might hurt you?'' More than one-fourth (28 percent) answered yes. Of this group 32 percent were girls and 23 percent boys. For both questions the number of girls reporting being fearful was slightly higher than the number of boys.

Violence inflicted on children by their own parents also seems to contribute to crime-related fears. Children who reported that their parents spanked them and yelled at them were more likely to be afraid of attackers and intruders than children who did not report such punishment.

Regardless of the exact figures, for far too many youngsters the fear of being hurt on the streets or in the playgrounds is not merely the result of childish imagination but a realistic response to their environment. Mean and violent behavior figures in their lives—perhaps more so than many adults are willing to recognize. To the question, "Who is the person you are most afraid of?" one child in five named a specific person or persons from their school or neighborhood who had hurt or threatened them in the past.

Fifteen percent of children in the United States, according to the Zill study, live in areas where parents say local crime is a problem. An additional 20 percent live in neighborhoods where their parents report there are "undesirable people in the streets, parks or playgrounds, such as drunks, drug addicts or tough older kids." But even in the so-called good neighborhoods, being harassed or threatened while playing is too frequent an experience to be dismissed.

Over half the children reported having been bothered by other children or by adults while they were playing outdoors. Forty-three percent said they had been harassed by older children and nearly 13 percent had been bothered by adults. More than one-third reported that they had been threatened with a beating; 12 percent said they had actually been beaten up. A ball or a similar item had been taken by force from one-fourth of the children; 5 percent said they had been robbed of money.

These events naturally affect children's perceptions about their environment. More than one child in six mentioned fighting, bullying, meanness, vandalism or crime as the thing they would most like to change about their neighborhood. They report that "people steal" and "people are mean." Some wishes for change have particular poignancy: "Stop older kids from fighting and picking on little kids" . . . "Get bicycles for all of us who got one stolen."

Most neighborhood incidents such as those described in the survey are not reported to the police. They do not appear in official crime statistics. The usual exceptions are when a bike is stolen or a serious assault takes place. Sometimes parents are reluctant to report even those. Children themselves may not even report many so-called minor incidents to their parents. But no matter how minor the incident may appear to an adult, it contributes to a child's overall sense of fear.

Even older students are known to have been adversely affected. The biggest worry of high school seniors, more than nuclear war or pollution, was found to be crime, according to another continuing study called *Monitoring the Future*, by the Institute for Social Research at the University of Michigan.

In a follow-up survey done in 1981 of 1,400 of the same children, now 12 to 16 years old, Dr. Zill found that crime-related fears were still present as children got older, even though a lower percentage reported them. To the question, "Do you feel afraid that somebody might break into your house?" 31 percent said yes in contrast to 68 percent when they were younger. Even at age 16, more than one-fourth were afraid that someone might force his way into their homes. While there was a drop from the earlier figure, virtually one-third of the teenagers remained fearful. The figures were higher for girls than boys.

When asked again, "Do you feel afraid when you go out that someone might hurt you?" 17 percent of the older children answered yes. A higher percentage of girls was afraid than boys. As indicated, there was some dropping off with age, but not a really substantial decline until ages 15 and 16.

Teenagers continue to report being bothered in their

neighborhoods. Again the numbers are smaller, but the problem remains.

## TV's Scary Messages

Young children get video messages early, sometimes with strange results. When our friends, parents of a five-year-old girl, told her that her grandmother had died, the little girl's first question was, "Who shot her?"

The overwhelming presence of violence on the home screen and its distortion of real life further complicate parents' efforts to teach children how to deal with the world in the safest and most rational manner. The prevalence of televised crime and violence and the frequency of portraying aggressive acts, especially in programs aimed at, or regularly watched by children, present a real problem. By the time the average child graduates from high school, he or she will have seen more than 13,000 violent deaths on the small screen by current estimates.

By homogenizing age groups, television treats young children as if they were grown up; they are part of a large common audience. Consequently, even young children can appear to be quite sophisticated about major issues, including violence and crime. How they absorb and handle the information they get from television is another matter, as the five-year-old in the story illustrates. Television lets children enter into experiences they never would have had before the days of video. But exposure is one thing and understanding quite another.

In a society saturated with television, the question must be asked, Does it play a role in making children and young people more afraid of crime than they otherwise would be? The answer, according to researchers in the field, seems to be affirmative. The more television children watch, the more crime-related fears they will have. "The fear that 'somebody bad might get into the house,' reported earlier by Dr. Zill, is so widespread among American children that it cuts across all economic groups. "The influence of television is certainly a factor," he says.

There is evidence linking television to children's fears. When they were asked, "Do you feel afraid of TV programs where people fight and shoot guns?" nearly one-fourth of the children responded yes. It is mostly youngsters aged seven and eight who say they are frightened by violent programs. "Many parents are surprised that elementary school children are still frightened by television programs, thinking this stops at a younger age," says Dr. Zill. In another survey, by the National Center for Health Statistics, 27 percent of the mothers in the sample reported that their children's sleep was disturbed by seeing certain television programs or movies.

There is a direct correlation in Dr. Zill's survey between the amount of time children spend watching television on the usual weekday and the children's reports of crime-related fears. Children described as heavy viewers (who watched three hours or more each day) were more likely to say they were afraid of intruders and attackers than children who spent less time in front of the television set. Even when there are controls for family background differences and actual crime incidence, heavy viewers are still more fearful than light viewers and nonviewers.

Television research by the Yale University husband-and-wife team Jerome and Dorothy Singer further confirms the finding that children who are heavy viewers, especially of violent action-filled programs, overestimate how frightening the real world is. These TV bred young viewers believe there is more crime in their neighborhoods than actually exists. "Some are even scared to ride their bikes," Dorothy Singer says.

"Television is the first mass-produced environment into which all children are born and in which they will live from cradle to grave," according to Dr. George Gerbner, dean of the Annenberg School of Communications at the University of Pennsylvania. Dr. Gerbner, an authority on the social impact of television beyond the children and violence arguments, has studied more than the link between violence on the screen and crime in the streets. The power of the medium over what we all think and learn, he believes, is comparable to the pervasive influence of the medieval church. The television screen provides a constant learning environment, especially for children.

Television explains the world and our common culture to us. It constructs a reality of its own. Its picture of what exists shows what its creators consider important and how they see a variety of ideas and events being related. Children often get their view of how the world works from watching television. And not only from children's programs. Experts point out that after the age of six only 20 percent of a child's viewing time is spent watching children's programs.

The television world, however, is not like the real world. Its distortions and exaggerations contribute to shallow and false perceptions. For example, on the small screen crime occurs about 10 times more often than it does in real life. Fifty-five percent of prime time TV characters are involved in violent confrontations once a week. In real life, the incidence of violence is a small fraction of that. In television's world four-fifths of all prime time and weekend daytime programs contain violence and two-thirds of all major characters are affected by it. During weekend and daytime children's programs, the rate of involvement in violence is even greater—a shocking 80 percent. While the networks average six violent acts per hour during prime time, Saturday morning children's cartoon shows average around 27, according to Dr. Gerbner's research.

Entertainment programs are not alone in causing problems; watching television news can present pitfalls for younger viewers. Though quite remote from most children's daily lives, accidents, murders, fires and riots receive a disproportionate share of time on the news and are therefore magnified in children's consciousness. And children can be scared seeing adults hurting others or destroying property.

Some parents have reported to Dorothy and Jerome Singer that their children have had nightmares after watching the news. In addition, there is no way to keep from children such frightening news events as the Atlanta killings or the disappearance of Etan Patz. Seeing and hearing these grim stories on television can magnify a child's fears unless parents are present and ready to put things into perspective.

## How to Reduce the Negative Effects of Television

1. Limit the amount of television children can watch without an adult present.
2. Set aside some regular viewing times to watch television with your children so you can discuss anything frightening.
3. Tell your child which programs you like and dislike and why.
4. Use news programs as openings for talks about any subject that is troubling to bring up.
5. Talk with your child about a program's content and concepts to make sure he or she understands what's going on.
6. Make sure you select particular programs to watch rather than just seeing any program that is on when you turn on the set.

The widely publicized cases of serious violence which seem to have been influenced directly by television programs or movies are rare, Dr. Gerbner states. It may well be true that the overwhelming majority of children are not rendered violent by television, but they are harmfully affected in other ways. The majority of children who are heavy viewers, Dr. Gerbner says, are learning how to be victims by watching TV violence, not how to be aggressors. They become more anxious and insecure and are more concerned about being victims of violence than children who do not watch as much television.

In summary, the results of surveys of adults and children by Dr. Gerbner and his colleagues confirmed that violence-laden television not only may cultivate aggressive tendencies in a minority but, perhaps more important, may generate a pervasive and an exaggerated sense of danger and mistrust. When asked about their chances of being involved in some kind of violence, heavy viewers responded in terms more characteristic of the television world than of the real world.

Surveys of adolescents also conducted by Dr. Gerbner and his colleagues at the Annenberg School of Communications, extend these findings. Teenagers in New York and New Jersey schools who are heavy viewers were more likely than light viewers to overestimate the number of people involved in violence and the proportion of people who commit serious crimes.

Most of the New Jersey students, about 80 percent, felt that it was dangerous to walk alone in a city at night. Within every comparison group, heavy viewers believed this more readily than light viewers. Although most students considered it dangerous, there was a greater chance that heavy viewers would express this fear. Responses to a question about willingness to walk alone at night in one's own neighborhood showed a strong and consistent relationship between the amount of viewing and the expression of fear.

In addition, Dr. Gerbner and his associates found that

television viewing also seems to contribute to adolescent as-
sumptions about law enforcement procedures and activities.
Among the New Jersey students, more heavy than light
viewers in every subgroup believed that the police must
often use force at a scene where there has been violence.
Among the New York students, there was a consistent, positive relationship between the amount of viewing and the perception of how many times a day a policeman pulls out a
gun.

Finally, adolescents who are heavy users also tended to
express general mistrust of others and to believe most people
were selfish. The amount of TV viewing made a constant
difference in the responses of the students tested, no matter
what their backgrounds.

The impact of television on a child's world cannot be exaggerated. By the time they graduate from high school, most
children will have spent more hours in front of the television
set than in the classroom. Experts will continue to debate the
degree to which children are harmed and their outlook distorted by television. But no one can seriously argue that
watching television makes our children feel safer.

Perhaps the only exceptions are those children for whom
coming home to a television set is physically safer than
being on the streets of an unsafe neighborhood. Some parents understandably prefer that their young children (ages
five to eight) come home directly from school and safely
watch television.

"Who can blame these parents?" asked the first-grade
teachers in Queens, New York, who told me about this practice and the views of the pupils' parents. The teachers had
noticed that youngsters in the classroom were restless and
unable to sit still for any period of time. When they investi-
gated, they found that at home these children were sitting in
front of TV sets, rarely getting exercise or fresh air.

But for the majority of children, the pervasive presence of television means that in addition to their own life experiences, they are having some frightening messages beamed at them, making them more fearful than they might otherwise be. In addition, they may be learning to play the role of victim just as readily as they may see themselves as potential aggressors. Children who are heavy viewers tend to be fearful of the real world. Because much of the earlier research about the impact of television focused on the degree to which it fostered aggressive behavior, this significant aspect has not been given the attention it deserves.

Television plays a vital role in shaping or misshaping children's perceptions of reality. Some researchers have found that while children do not seem to confuse TV with the things they know from their own experience, it may distort their ideas about people and places outside their knowledge. Parents should not be misled by their children's television-induced sophistication about crime and violence—or any other subject. Children often seem to "know" much more than they really understand.

Three elements—actual experience of street crime, news media reports about crime and television entertainment which deals with crime—are all connected and reinforce each other. The first two are real problems which must be dealt with pragmatically and sensibly. But the third is also a factor in our children's environment that parents must acknowledge. While the first two can be dealt with directly, the general impact of television entertainment is harder to locate and confront. But it has an influence on our children's safety thinking which needs sensible discussion and explanations as much as the others to minimize and diffuse any potential harm.

Since moderate television viewers are not as adversely affected as heavy viewers, the message is obvious. In addition, if parents can be active participants in the lives of their children, if they can provide positive experiences for their youngsters—and help minimize the negative ones—the adverse effects of television violence can be made negligible.

## Crime: Myth versus Reality

"What you have now is a very realistic sense on the part of people that life is not the same as it was 20 years ago. I think people's perceptions of crime are grounded in very hard reality. Their cars are being stolen, their kids are being mugged, their apartments are being burglarized. Do any of us know a family who has not had a bicycle taken? Who has not had a car broken into for the radio, the stereo or the car itself? Who has not had an apartment or a home burglarized? Who has not been mugged or had a friend who was mugged on the street?"

These are not the words of an upset parent. This is New York City's former Police Commissioner Robert H. McGuire talking. And what he says is true for cities across the nation.

The petty crime our children face used to be considered an urban problem, confined to bad neighborhoods. It was often the reason for moving to the suburbs. Today it happens everywhere, even in so-called good neighborhoods. Bikes are stolen in affluent suburbs. Front doors as well as cars are kept locked—and with good reason.

When I was growing up, it was rare for anyone to know personally the victim of a robbery. I rode the New York subways without fear. When I went to college during the 1950s, I did not have to lock the door to my room every time I left the dormitory; my son, now in college, cannot afford such a luxury. His roommate recently foiled a burglar's attempt.

There are other differences between the time of my childhood and life today. Most of us then used to feel relatively safe from the random violence that has more recently been bred by the quest for money to buy drugs. In addition, the proliferation of deadly weapons has become a fact of life for all Americans. Today just about everyone either has been the victim of a crime or knows someone who has.

And so do our children. Chances are that one of their friends has been involved in an unpleasant incident, at the very least, even if they themselves have not. Today children are as exposed to attacks as adults. While gangs are responsible for some trouble, it is just as likely to come from individuals—young, roving, unpredictable and ever-present. They prey on girls as well as boys.

Contrary to popular perception, the young rather than the elderly are the most frequent victims of violent crimes and thefts, according to current research. "Kids prey on kids more than they prey on the elderly," says Jim Cartier of the Juvenile Justice Center in San Marcos, Texas. The most common scenario is a youngster being pushed against a lavatory wall in school, having his or her lunch money stolen under threat of violence.

Young people aged 12 to 24 had the highest victimization rate in crimes of violence or theft, and those 65 and over had the lowest, according to a recent Justice Department Victimization Survey. Males aged 12 to 24 are especially vulnerable to robbery, assault or personal larceny; they had higher rates than men or women in any older-age category.

There is good reason to worry about crime and to recognize that it can touch all of us. Since the end of World War II, the crime rate has climbed steeply. According to the Uniform Crime Reports of the Federal Bureau of Investigation, the chances of being the victim of a major violent crime such as murder, rape, robbery or aggravated assault nearly tripled between 1960 and 1976, as did the probability of being the victim of a serious crime against property such as burglary, auto theft or purse snatching.

During the early 1980s the crime rate rise has appeared to level off, with some years showing slight decreases. But overall criminal activity remains at a high level. Moreover, crime in rural areas and outer suburbs across the nation rose faster than in the cities in the 1970s according to FBI figures. "In their persistent efforts to escape the cities, Americans have opened up the countryside to some of the same forces that historically brought crime to the core of large urban areas—a transient, restless population, an influx of poor immigrants from other regions and impersonal relationships that make it easier for a person to steal."

The increase in crime in rural areas and outlying suburbs, according to many authorities, is one reason that national crime rates began to soar during the 1970s. Many parents who moved from the cities to escape their problems have found that the problems have moved along with them.

President Reagan has called crime "an American epidemic" which touches roughly one-third of all American homes. A Justice Department report released in April 1981 states that a "large minority of American households experience crime each year, though most of them experience it in nonviolent forms. There is great stability in the patterns from year to year."

Fear of crime continues to pervade our society; 45 percent of Americans are afraid to go out alone at night within a mile of their homes, according to a 1983 Gallup poll. And in urban areas, 76 percent of the women polled feared walking alone at night in their neighborhoods. The poll findings reflected a widely held belief that the actual crime situation in the country is more serious than official Government figures indicate "because many incidents are not reported to the police."

No matter what variations occur in crime reporting, the statistics are not reassuring. A study by a private research group found that crime-related fear has become so "alarmingly pervasive'' that it has changed the way many people live in our country.

Fears of becoming a crime victim have led many people to buy handguns and many others to think about purchasing them. How many guns actually have been bought is not officially known, but expert estimates put the number at between 35 and 50 million.

The question is: Can a gun be an effective tool in preventing crime? Will it keep you and your children safe?

All of the law enforcement representatives I consulted agree that as a safety device a gun is more of a menace than a protection. Former Commissioner McGuire stated publicly that statistics show ''when people carry guns, they're very much more at risk than the victim of crime who does not possess a gun.'' Inspector Jim Humphrey of the Crime Prevention Unit in the Detroit Police Department said emphatically he did not advocate guns for home protection: ''Most people who have guns don't know how to use them. They are six times more likely to use a gun mistakenly against a relative or friend than an intruder.''

In the case of robbery, the element of surprise is in the criminal's favor. Few robbery victims, even if they own a gun, are able to get to it fast enough. A friend of ours who surprised a thief entering his home and scared him off asked a police officer afterward what would have happened had he owned a gun. ''You might very well be dead now,'' the policeman replied. ''If you had said, 'Stop or I'll shoot,' you would have waited, but the burglar would not. He would have shot you.''

. Studies show that unarmed victims are less likely to be injured or killed by robbers than those who brandish weapons. Crime prevention experts suggest that except in very unusual situations a person who owns a gun should not try to act the hero to protect property. Moreover, accidental deaths caused by the possession of guns in the home are four times more numerous than those caused by robbers and burglars, according to former U.S. Attorney General Edward Levi.

Detective Jack Meeks of New York City's Crime Prevention Section adds his strong views on guns and children: "If you have kids, do not keep a gun in the house." A detective for 17 years and the father of four children, he is a police officer who has made his share of arrests. But as soon as he gets home, he says: "I unload the gun. I put a lock through it and put it away. The ammunition is separated from the gun. The gun is locked, so even if you found the ammunition you couldn't put the bullets into it and make it fire."

"Guns and kids don't mix under any circumstances. With a gun, there can't be any mistakes. Just don't have one. Don't teach kids anything about them. Just say guns are bad. Adults can make choices. They can exercise some control, but a child has none."

Crime prevention officers address many community groups. One told me that he once had a man in the audience with a six-year-old and this man said he kept a gun handy. This father illustrates a problem the police can encounter, a parent who shows his son a gun, tells him how deadly it is and warns him never to go near it.

"As nicely as I could, I told this man he was out of his mind," the police officer said. "His boy was only six. All his son has to do is forget one time and he blows his head off. Kids are allowed to make mistakes when they are six. But he could be dead or someone else might be. I really get mad at this. You can teach kids things and they forget and it's ok, but not with a gun."

While a father who shows his six-year-old his loaded gun is not being smart, we can sympathize with his desire to protect his child. Some parents, scared by all the crime news, might do the same. But there are better responses than going out and buying a gun.

One is, of course, to teach children safe behavior in different situations. They need to learn how to protect themselves from people and events that can harm them. Failure to teach children how to behave in unsafe situations makes them even more vulnerable. But an awareness of danger and crime does not have to mean that we or our children should live in fear.

We must teach them to be optimistic and to learn the difference between real dangers and imagined ones that cause panic or despair. Yes, there is good reason for caution on the streets. Still, the fact is that more crimes are directed against property than against people. While we do not like being robbed of our possessions, ultimately they are less important than our persons.

It is difficult to reconcile the contradiction in teaching our children to be trusting, helpful and caring and, at the same time, alerting them that not everyone can be trusted. Unfortunately, the good and bad guys are not always as neatly identified as in Western movies or on television; so we sometimes make mistakes. We cannot entirely eliminate this predicament, but we can try to judge situations realistically and teach our children to do the same.

We help our family, friends and acquaintances as much as possible. We help those we do not know personally in our communities by building stronger ties in our neighborhoods. When people work together and help each other, unknown factors are reduced, fears lessen and everyone feels safer.

# ■ 2 ■

# Make Safety
# Family Policy

SINCE the beginning of time, children have wanted to explore the world and parents have warned them about its pitfalls. This is a classic theme, often the core of children's literature and fairy tales. The universal parental warning about the dangers of talking to a stranger, for example, is a central part of one of the most famous of all fairy tales, Little Red Riding Hood.

But in earlier days, the rules drawn up for children were simpler and there were fewer of them. The risks were of a different nature. Children could be given greater leeway in asserting their independence and exercising judgment. A few rules covered most situations. Today general rules cannot be stretched to cover all possible dangerous grounds. Parents must constantly try to come up with guidelines for new and changing risks in a child's daily life. Children even need safety rules for inside school, once considered a safe place.

Parents, especially in cities, often feel a sense of inadequacy about their ability to protect their children, says Dr.

Karolynn Siegel, a researcher who has studied how families reacted to safety-related stress. With her colleague, Carol Kunzel, at the Center for Policy Research in New York City, she interviewed parents at the Bank Street School in New York City. They found certain themes that trouble parents everywhere, though they are felt more acutely in cities.

Family stress often results when parents, usually reluctantly, create an elaborate fabric of "don't do" or "don't go" admonitions for their children, trying to cover every situation a child might encounter, from dealing with phone calls at home to handling incidents on public buses. In such an all-inclusive "system," the restrictions are hard on both parents and children. In a more positive vein, one out of ten parents studied said that in addition to rules they had, on their own initiative, identified shopkeepers on their children's school routes where the youngsters could go if they were in trouble.

A problem that emerged from this study is the inevitable conflict between parents' instinctive wish to teach children they can trust the world and its people and the need to teach children to be wary of danger and become street smart. Parents quite naturally worry that children may be hurt if they are not taught to be mindful of potential dangers; but most parents, like those in the survey, are also sensitive to implicit messages when they teach a child to be vigilant. They worry that they may be teaching children that the world is hostile and dangerous and the only safe way to cope is to withdraw and hide in their shells. They dislike saying, "We have to be careful when we drive through certain neighborhoods" or "We can't let anyone into our house we do not know."

During the time Drs. Siegel and Kunzel were doing their study, the disappearance of six-year-old Etan Patz was in the news. Many of the parents brought up the case when they were being interviewed. They identified with the boy's mother when she was quoted as saying, "If I had walked Etan to the bus stop, he'd still be here." They were thinking about their own children. Their fears were reflected in their talk about little Etan. It is natural for parents everywhere with a child near the same age to think, "What if he had been my child?" Many became less secure and were asking themselves whether their children were ready to be given added independence and how much. When there is a dramatic incident, parents are frequently moved to ask themselves, "Did I give my child independence too soon?" Even lesser occurrences can give vent to parents' self-recrimination; they wonder, "Should I have waited another year?"

Many of the study participants reported they had changed their daily routines because of their perception of crime lurking around the corner and not only under the influence of the Patz case. They had either experienced unpleasant incidents with their children or heard about bad experiences from friends, perhaps not with any serious consequences, but frightening all the same. They did not necessarily like their new fearful attitudes, but could not shake off their uneasiness.

Now these parents were less likely to send a child out alone on an errand in the early evening. With younger children of eight or nine, they resumed responsibility for walking them to school and picking them up in the afternoon. They planned to continue the practice for longer than they had envisioned previously. Earlier, they might have wanted to encourage independence; now they were not so sure. Often, they would hesitate to leave a second child home alone at night as young as they had deemed all right with their first.

Another complicating problem for all parents which came out in the survey is racial distrust. The fear of crime keeps racial prejudice alive. Avoidance of certain neighborhoods is a routine practice. Many parents identified blacks and Hispanics as aggressors and stated as a fact that these groups furnish a disproportionately high number of attackers and muggers.

Such racial prejudice manifested itself only in one-to-one interviews; it was not expressed in group discussions where both blacks and whites were represented. Even though the Bank Street School, on Manhattan's Upper West Side, is known for its liberal attitudes, many parents were still not able to shed their view of racial stereotypes.

The black parents interviewed had their own problems. They felt generally that black boys are more often the victims of violence than black girls. This is because males are more often the focus of hostility and suspicion than females, rather than for any underlying sexual reason. Actually, black children are more often subject to attack both in predominantly black and in predominantly white neighborhoods.

The responses of the parents in this study show just a few of the racial and ethnic aspects involved in street crime. Distrust between different groups is an unfortunate side effect. Whites often feel that blacks and Hispanics are prone to violence. There is no ignoring the fact that one of the first questions usually asked after white middle-class people are mugged is, "Was he black?" When they talk about their adventures on the street, white boys often admit that they are more cautious when they run into a group of blacks.

This is a tough issue for parents who want to raise their children free of racial prejudice. There is no easy answer to this aspect of street crime either for us or for our children. As long as crime rates remain high, racial distrust will continue to be a sad consequence. The best course is to be honest about your own feelings and beliefs. A child will sense them anyway. Parents must approach this delicate issue in a way that suits their general outlook, using ideas and words they are comfortable with. Children can be told that poverty has always been a breeding ground for street crime, and as long as poverty affects certain groups disproportionately, there will also be a disproportionate number from the group who break the law. Children at an early age can be made to understand that while crime cannot be condoned, it is everybody's duty to help eliminate discrimination and other conditions that keep some groups in poverty.

Talking about another aspect of her research, Dr. Siegel, a psychologist, considered the possible effects of street crime on children's overall development.

*One unfortunate consequence is that it is harder to develop a sense of independence. Between the ages of six and eleven is when children should be working on separating from their parents and developing their own sense of mastery over their environment. This is just the time when the conditions of the street can force them into greater dependence on their parents and on other adults.*

*Moreover, the advice "when someone bigger on the street asks you for something give it to them" may be sensible from a safety viewpoint, but it can make a child feel helpless and passive. These feelings can carry over to other areas of life as well, with negative results.*

*The parents we studied, aware of the high crime rate, are hovering over their children more than they might have in the past. One risk involved is that the independence children work toward during this stage of the life cycle is being postponed because it might compromise their safety. But it is important for youngsters to develop this sense of their own competence over their world. Parents should be aware of this developmental need so they can balance it against children's safety needs. Then neither will be neglected.*

Most city parents agree that children cannot explore their surroundings in the same way as some of their country cousins, but living in an urban apartment house means that city children do meet a more heterogeneous group of people than their counterparts in suburbia.

What seems sensible to many urban parents is a gradual transition and step-by-step increase in a child's responsibility. When city children are old enough to cross streets, their lives suddenly change. Horizons widen. A new world opens up. It is the first step to gradual independence—moving freely on the streets. For elementary school children, once given the ready sign, it means being able to go and buy their own candy or pick up orange juice for the family.

One mother who has brought up her children in the city and swears it is a healthy environment for them cites the advantages of increased opportunities through mobility. She is convinced that youngsters who grow up on urban pavements are more independent than their surburban counterparts, who depend on their parents as chauffeurs when they visit a friend or go to the movies. Once a city child is allowed to use public transportation, the city becomes a place filled with wonderful things to do. Suburban youngsters do not catch up until they learn to drive and can afford their own cars.

Some suburban children who do not know city life occasionally develop lurid ideas about that strange world beyond their sheltered one. When we spent a summer in Stanford, California, an older boy who was playing with our younger son, then eight, expressed surprise that John was not afraid of getting shot when he went out on the streets of New York. Even adults outside the bigger cities regularly express disbelief that people there—including children—play and walk in the parks.

A friend, who lived in the suburbs outside New York City before she moved into town, described how she handled her teenage son's urban street education. For a while, he traveled with a city-bred friend who taught him what to do and what not to do. A bright student, he learned fast and taught his city friend some strategies for getting ahead in school. "Each boy had his own turf," my friend said, "his own area of expertise. I let my son go out with his city friends quite reluctantly at first, but I relaxed when I saw how my plan was working. When kids are older, I think there is a need for other kids to do the teaching in this kind of situation. Sometimes they do not "hear" their parents.

Almost as an afterthought she added, "I don't think I'd have taken the risk with a girl." Many parents, much as they would like to feel different, would undoubtedly share her beliefs.

## Speaking Out about Safety

Telling children about the disturbed men and women who may prey on unwary youngsters is one of a parent's most distasteful tasks. It is a hard subject to discuss, but it is part of the job of being a parent.

The first thing to remember is that this is not a "one time" subject. You will not be able to have one big talk and get it over with in the way that the Victorians pictured teaching about sex. The subject of threats to personal safety is as difficult to discuss as sex and, because of the negative overtones, perhaps even harder. Many parents are therefore tempted to ignore the subject in the hope that things will work out by themselves, eliminating the need for discussion.

But ignoring the subject puts children at a serious disadvantage. That is why it pays to take time and use the proper occasions to talk over different aspects of street safety. Once you have recognized that one big "facts of life" session will not do the trick, continuous communication, which should be your goal, is under way. In fact, one discussion would not even be good for just giving the "facts" or your rules. In this, as in other things to learn, most children will not be able to absorb all the information at once.

By pouring out an overwhelming number of facts and rules, you run the risk of scaring a child. One mother with two little girls, ages five and seven, reported that after her first talk about safety, the girls were so frightened that they would not go outside the house for a week. She has since learned how to get her message across more calmly and with greater assurance so that she does not frighten her daughters.

Remember that you are not just transmitting information. You are dealing with attitudes about life and the world. These are important overtones you will be communicating whether you are aware of it or not. Over a period of time, as you talk gradually about personal safety, you will give your child an awareness of the issues which are part of the lives of all of us.

To make your task easier, accent what children can do to protect themselves, not what scares them. Stress the positive aspects of safety and make children feel competent as early as possible. Essentially, parents should treat the threat of street dangers as something to be mastered. Then children will develop more savvy and self-confidence. It is possible to warn them of the dangers they may find when they go out alone without scaring them half to death.

"The two biggest fears for children and teenagers are death and humiliation," says psychologist Steven Levenkron, affiliated with Montefiore Hospital in New York. "When kids or adolescents come into a hospital, these are their two main fears. We think of them as street fears—and they are—but I don't think kids are as aware of them on the streets as they are if you put them into a hospital; yet the fears are present whether they are expressed or not."

## Six FALSE Beliefs about Personal Safety

1. Talking about dangers will scare children.
2. Fear in children is all bad.
3. What they don't know can't hurt them.
4. Nothing bad can happen in our neighborhood.
5. Self-protection is based on physical skill and athletic ability.
6. Having a bad experience will make a child tougher and stronger.

"It's not just teens and kids. In fact, most of us have fears of being left alone or being physically harmed or humiliated or killed. These are the fears we can identify.

"I think kids are more in touch with feeling powerless than adults are, even though they share some of the same fears. Children experience more powerlessness in their lives than adults do, with fewer compensations. An adult, for example, may feel powerless at work, but not at home. Children experience powerlessness in all aspects of their lives, and particularly in regard to adults and the adult world. They engage, therefore, in many power struggles with their peers, which to us may seem meaningless unless we view them against this background."

The big task for children—developing mastery over their environment—is learned very gradually. But children can be taught certain survival precepts as the need arises: to avoid certain places, not to be out during certain hours, etc. If they are taught these things, if the message comes from the parent that we have to accept and observe certain rules to be able to live where we are, that there are benefits to living in our particular area as well as disadvantages, then children will learn positively without anger and with less fear. To be alert to certain facts becomes a part of life in a simple and straightforward manner.

If we are willing to come to grips with the reality that there is some danger around us and say in a matter-of-fact manner "because there is danger it is only common sense to take the following precautions," we are teaching our children to be street smart. We are teaching them competence. These lessons are taught as part of mastering the environment and are communicated in that fashion, just as certain survival skills are taught in summer camp. Children will then learn whatever they need to know. On the other hand, if the instruction reflects only the parents' fear, a child may rebel and do reckless things just to prove the parents wrong.

Whether you are bringing up a child in a city or suburb, you can provide a continuing set of instructions, not ones given fearfully at the last minute. We say to a younger child, for example, "When you are playing in front of the house, you may not cross the street unless I cross with you." Such instructions are not given on an emergency basis; they are repeated day-in, day-out over a period of time, until the child follows them as a matter of course, understanding that they represent a parent's caring not punishment.

Actually, such teaching is really part of establishing family policy. Much that governs children's lives is taught—or ought to be—as family policy and thus is easier to remember and follow. We say in effect, "Look, it is not our family policy for a young girl or boy to be out on the street alone after 9 o'clock at night because of the greater risks involved. If you are coming home that late, you must be accompanied by two or three other people."

Trouble starts when the parents wait until the child is reaching for the doorknob to say something such as, "Don't go out, it's after 8 o'clock. I'm worried something may happen to you." Your child's impulse is to reply, "Nothing will happen" and then rush out the door. Lack of advance instruction and a permanent structure tends to lead to impulsive disregard of last-minute improvised objections.

If you have had earlier policy talks with your child, you would just say, "We have an understanding about 8 o'clock" (or 9 o'clock or whatever the agreed-upon time may be). The child might still try to bargain, "Yeah, but . . ." You, however, then are in a prearranged position to reply, "Sit down, let's discuss it." You are on much stronger ground. If you feel that it is unsafe to modify your basic rule, if your child is still too young, if there is no group for him or her to come home with, you will have to stick to the original agreement.

If you are concerned about a particular neighborhood, or if you live in the city and worry about the subway as a means of transportation, you will want to declare it off limits. When the question is about going to a friend's house after school, you will want to discuss a certain agreed-upon time for your child's return.

You have started out with "You can't cross the street" and progressed to "You can cross the street now," but other sensible restrictions still remain. Each stage in your child's development leads to a new level of the policy that governs your child's whereabouts. You gradually increase the youngster's responsibilities. Many children ask for more responsibility before parents feel they are ready to handle it. This has to be worked out on an individual basis. If there is a background of family policy, the transitions will be easier to negotiate.

But there are always legitimate limits. For example, a girl of any age should not be allowed to be out at 2:00 A.M. or to travel alone all around a city—a dangerous practice even for adult women. The limits get modified as a child grows older and greater discretion is shifted to the child. Your child should never get to a point where he or she feels there is no danger at all, because there will always be some. It is a good idea to point out that adults have some safety parameters, too, that you do not walk city streets at 3 A.M. or drive in certain deserted areas after midnight if you can avoid it. Parents of a teenage boy found this reminder effective when they were discussing what time he should come home after a party.

As your child grows older, the tone and content of your conversations change. And it is important to keep communications open during and after the elementary school years. You can keep pointing out that as adults you do not do everything you want or go everywhere you want. There are places to which you do not go alone—or after dark. By doing this, you have defined your own limits. Parents must listen to their own advice. Does it sound fair or hypocritical? Children can easily discern hypocrisy. This is one area where do what I say, not what I do, simply will not work.

The matter of trust is crucial. Take the question, "When are you coming home?" or the admonition "Be home by 6 o'clock." To a 10-year-old, this may sound as if you don't trust him. How do you counter this? Again, it is not a one-time thing. Your child should be used to hearing you yourself say when you will be coming home and also to your phoning when you are delayed. By what you yourself do, you teach your children to abide by family rules and to respect them because they are not discriminatory. You are not making special rules for them merely because they are younger and less powerful. We all live by rules. They are not just for children. Having certain family rules increases our safety. You are saying "This is the way we all do things in our home. We may not like all the rules we live by. We may be sorry that they are necessary, but we have to live by them all the same."

This does not mean that all problems will thus be eliminated. As children get older, they want to test the rules you have made by breaking them, at the same time testing their power and independence. Sometimes, after your question, "What time will you be home?" they may ask, "What's the

matter, don't you trust us?'' The answer can be no, sometimes you don't trust them automatically and without question. In other words, you are justified in asking, ''Are you
really going to be home at 11 o'clock or are you going somewhere and smoke pot?'' The question, in fact, relates not
just to when they will be coming home, but to what they
may be doing. It is good to keep that in mind—as your pre-
rogative and parental duty.

Parents ought to address the reality about children's activities, advises Dr. Edward A. Davies, head of Pediatrics at
Lenox Hill Hospital in New York. ''Do not say, 'It's too
late for you to be out.' It will only invite an argument. 'No,
it's not too late for me to be out. All the other kids are going
to be out that late.'

''Just state your concerns openly. 'I don't know if at that
party they're going to smoke pot or have a lot of booze. And
I think you're too young to handle this. Can you tell me
that's not going to happen?''

In another example, say with a 13-year-old, what you
need to do, Dr. Davies suggests, is to expose him to reality,
not hide him from it. He wants to come home from somebody's party alone. The first question to ask is, ''How are
you going to do that? Are you going to take a cab? Will you
be able to get one? Will you walk? Take a bus? In short, Are
you going to feel comfortable doing it?''

Dr. Davies continues: ''The real question parents must
ask finally is 'Can you tell me how you are going to get
home? Do you feel comfortable and safe, because it could
be unpleasant?' If they say, 'I feel fine. I can take care of
myself,' you can say, 'All right. Go ahead and do it.'

''Don't get into a you're-too-young-to-go-out-that-late
type of argument. You need to be much more frank. You
can say, 'I'm really worried about your safety in getting
home.' '' Some parents hesitate to raise such questions for
fear of making children afraid. But the idea is to let a child

know what problems he might face in coming home alone. Sometimes a child is going to have to take a chance. Hopefully, he won't have an unpleasant experience. But at least, you have talked about it beforehand.

"Parents should talk about real issues, no matter how difficult these may be, when they talk to older children," Dr. Davies says. "None of this, 'It's not right for someone of your age to be out this late.' Then the child says, 'You are just trying to keep me a baby forever?' And your talk gets nowhere. Be more candid and talk about the real problem upfront."

In talking about limits for children, every parent must make an estimate of their neighborhood's relative safety. There is a difference in talking about New York City or St. Louis or a small town in the far West. Parents can gauge where safety begins and ends in their communities. There are still some places where people do not lock either their cars of their homes. And then there are others where people use double locks on every door and burglar alarms in their cars.

Suburbs are generally considered safer than big cities, but even there some sections are safer than others. When we spent summers living in Palo Alto, California, I consulted another mother to learn where it would be safe to let my son ride his bike alone and in which shopping centers he could spend time by himself wandering around without us. I knew even in this idyllic town there were some areas that would not be considered safe for a nine-year-old alone. And when we took a day trip to San Francisco, Paul would not be allowed to go off by himself. He was unhappy about this because there were places in New York where he could go without an adult; but San Francisco was a strange city. In an unknown area, it is not a good idea automatically to follow the rules established at home. We pointed out to him that he had greater freedom to ride his bike in Palo Alto than he had at home which would have to compensate for lesser freedom in a strange big city.

## Talking about Fears Is Important

Children must be taught safety rules the way they are taught to wash their hands before meals and to brush their teeth. Dangers do lurk in our streets and children must know how to deal with them. We need to tell them over and over again that if they take reasonable precautions the odds are good that they will be safe.

Along with good safety habits, your children need to know they can share with you whatever happens to them— the bad as well as the good. By talking about this difficult subject in a calm and confident manner and making it part of family policy and conversations, by taking the lead when they are small, you build the foundation of lifelong trust.

"The time for teaching safety measures is when children are young," says Detective Jack Meeks of the New York City Police Department's Crime Prevention Section, who organizes school safety presentations for kindergarten through third grade groups. "Children should learn how to handle themselves while they are in the first few years of school. Then by the time they do go out alone, they will have developed their instinctive security know-how."

You have already been teaching your preschooler not to touch a hot stove or run into the street. More complex safety instructions are a logical extension of such lessons. Starting early makes it easier to deal with your child at each age level. You know what they can absorb at every stage. It is neither necessary nor smart to tell small children any more than the simplest concrete instructions: "Don't go into the street" or "Wait for me to cross." But you should elaborate in appropriate ways, for example, by telling them not to run into the street even for a ball or a toy.

Young children think about danger a great deal, even if they don't talk about their fears to their parents. Detective Meeks says, ''They know there are dangers in their environment. They see a great deal of crime and violence on television and they hear about it from their friends.'' As psychiatrist Bruno Bettelheim has pointed out, small children are frequently unable to express their everyday fears in words, they can only do it by talking about fear of the dark or of some animal or some anxiety about the body. Fairy tales, popular through the ages, Bettelheim reminds us, depict dangers, violence and children's fears of helplessness, and they frequently offer imaginative solutions.

It requires tact and understanding for parents to help children cope with their fears. If dangers and anxieties are discussed openly, children learn how to handle situations they may have to face. Moreover, if coping with dangers is not discussed by parents, a trained school person or police officer, your child will seek information elsewhere. He or she may hear scary stories from friends or other parents. The information may not be either accurate or helpful—and it could unnecessarily frighten a child.

## Dealing with Fears

*DOs*

1. *Listen* to a child's fears in a calm manner.
2. *Respect* your child's fears. They help to protect him or her.
3. *Help* children overcome fears first by talking about them and then by teaching appropriate action.

*DON'Ts*
1.  Never make fun of fears.
2.  Never shame children in front of others because they are afraid.
3.  Don't become impatient and treat the child as if fears were babyish.
4.  Don't assume it is unnatural for a child to have some fears.
5.  Don't assume a safety problem that causes fears is your child's fault—or yours.

It is important to recognize that a child's fears can create discomfort in parents. This is why in some instances parents either deliberately or subconsciously try not to recognize children's fears. They may overlook them or even belittle a child's spoken fears in order to minimize their own anxiety. Some parents believe making light of a child's fears will alleviate them. Nothing could be further from the truth. Belittling a child's fears can make the child ashamed, in addition to being frightened.

Moreover, there are some hard-to-acknowledge aspects of teaching safety lessons. For example, a young child may be told, misleadingly, "If you are good and do what you are supposed to, you will always be safe." Yet the fact is that the child may be mugged or molested even if he or she is the best person in the world and does all the right things. Finding out that the assurances were false can make the experience doubly traumatic. In addition, it is hard for elementary school children to accept the idea that parents may not be omnipresent or strong enough to protect them from street hazards. There are realistic limits to a parent's capacity to protect, and children must be made quietly aware of this without fear of reducing parental authority. Twenty years ago, these limits did not register so early in a child's life and this may be disturbing to parents.

Some parents wonder whether discussions of possible dangers might frighten young children. Jane Richman of Evanston, Illinois, remembers that there were a few mothers who voiced such concerns before their children attended a special program called "Safety Town," sponsored by the local PTA. It was for young children starting school and it featured games and special art work. Afterward, even the most apprehensive mothers were pleased. "The children learned a lot," Mrs. Richman said. "When a trained school group talks about safety, even though they say the same things you do at home, it seems more official, even to little ones. My daughter was impressed and paid attention."

If the fears and dangers that may have to be confronted are presented openly, a child can learn how to handle them. It is hard to teach a young child not to answer when a stranger asks for the time or for directions; to keep on walking or even run away; never to get too close to a car when its passengers ask directions; never to open the front door without knowing who is outside; not to let any stranger come into the house or apartment to use the phone. (An alternative is to offer to make the call while the person waits safely outside.) It's all right to give our friends rides, but never to open the car to hitchhikers, no matter how nice they look.

It is sad to have to teach these things, but it is necessary.

All the experts I consulted agreed that it is crucial to have an advance understanding of potential risks and what a child can do to avert or at least minimize them. Some parents find it hard to face statistics that there is a strong probability a school-age child will encounter some unpleasant street incident. If you have not discussed street safety and a problem actually does occur, you may not be able to help your child as readily in the heat of the incident as if there had been some prior understanding of the risks all children and adults face.

Safety experts who conduct school assemblies report that

they always encounter children whose parents have not discussed the subject at home. In most cases the omission is
made with the best intentions or because the parents are
afraid to raise the subject. But such silence can be harmful.
Moreover, children are then less likely to report an unpleasant episode because they are embarrassed or even blame
themselves. Otherwise, they ask themselves, wouldn't Mom
and Dad have warned them? Many times in safety
assemblies children describe unpleasant incidents they have
not told anyone earlier.

If you don't know how or where to begin your talks, you
can wait for a natural opening to present itself. When you
are alert in looking for an opportunity, it will be easy to find.
You might begin with traffic safety while you and your child
are crossing the street. Or you may find a suitable occasion
while watching television with your children. (I did this with
my children and found it a good way to encourage communication about almost any subject; when a frightening situation appears on the screen or a person is threatened, you
have a natural opening. Television provides many such opportunities. (See Chapter 1.) Reading together will provide
others. After a school safety program, your child may have
additional questions or feelings to share with you. One father reported that his son had seen a Safe Harbor sticker on a
store window and asked what it meant. This was a perfect
time to talk about what the boy should do if he encountered
any trouble.

Sometimes a child's friend has had a bad experience
which will prove threatening or frightening to your child,
who may be thinking, ''What would I do if that happened to
me? How would I act? Would I be brave? Would I be safe?''
Encourage your child to talk as much as possible about these
fears even if they are expressed through another child's experiences.

Ironically, in order to create a climate of safety, it is necessary to accept a child's fears. Fear serves as a protection and young children need protection. The best way to handle a child's fears—or anyone's, including your own—is to start with the realization that fear is not always irrational. Children fear what might harm them and withdraw. Often, in primitive times, this running away was a lifesaving measure. In many cases today it can mean almost the same thing.

It is important for parents to recognize that they themselves have some fears. Having fears and recognizing them is not the same as being cowardly. We all know that some things in our world are dangerous. Only a fool would not admit this. What parents need to watch out for in themselves is not to go to the extreme of being either overly fearful or overly unconcerned. It is neither helpful to deny street dangers nor good to exaggerate them, any more than it is helpful to deny the existence of air pollution or other problems in our environment.

Parents, especially well-meaning ones, who spend a lot of time with their children, may often assume quite naturally that these children know more than they actually do. So certain practical things are often not spelled out sufficiently. Or abstract concepts are not made concrete enough for young children. Few are articulate enough to ask as one three-year-old did, "What does danger look like?"

Also, there is a need to say things more than once when you are talking about safety. Do not worry about repeating yourself. It is part of your teaching responsibility. Teachers understand the value of repetition. And it is important to check whether your children have understood what you are telling them. Nothing is sadder or more futile—or more unnecessary—than to hear a parent say after an incident, "But I told him not to do that."

Many adults, particularly middle-class parents, can find it difficult to teach children about personal safety because it means that they are teaching their children not to be "nice" to everybody all the time. But it is an important lesson for children, even at an early age. There are times and situations when being nice can be dangerous. This is especially true for girls, who are usually taught to be compliant and follow adult prescriptions, more than for boys.

When children are old enough to be out on their own, it becomes more important for them to be smart than to be indiscriminantly "nice." It is smart to be able to spot trouble and run away or not to answer when a stranger comes up to you and asks you the time. (Why would an adult ask a child the time anyway?)

### Some "Nice" Teachings to Be Followed Only at Home. On the Street, They Can Make Children More Vulnerable.

1. Always answer a question when you are asked.
2. When spoken to by an adult, always acknowledge the adult with a smile or an answer.
3. Always do what adults ask them to do.
4. Neither bother other people nor make a scene because someone is making them uncomfortable.
5. Always thank people for their kindness when they offer to help you.
6. Always be helpful and show compassion for people who are less fortunate than you.

It is vital to get across that the "nice" and trusting behavior a child has been carefully taught for family and friends does not apply to the streets. Such training—learning two different sets of behavior—need not be confusing to a child, if the need for it is clear in a parent's mind and is properly explained.

## What Do Other Parents Do?

Whether they live in cities or suburbs, parents are regularly besieged by their children's demands for greater freedom and increased privileges. Families must work out safety policy guidelines for their children based on their assessments of the individual child and neighborhood. What activities can be allowed with a reasonable degree of safety and when?

What do other parents do? That is what many perplexed families would like to know. Parents at the Trinity School in New York City wanted to find out. Since most of the school's parents did not know one another, the classic children's plea, "Everyone else is doing it," could be used effectively by students to stretch the rules and get their own way. On the rare occasions when parents were able to compare notes, they were surprised by the similarity of their experiences and their viewpoints.

In order to give parents a better idea of how other parents felt, the Trinity Parents Association sent a questionnaire to its families to discover what rules each home actually had established for its children. The response rate was high. More than half of all the parents answered the nine-page questionnaire.

The Trinity student body, while basically homogeneous, is multiracial and of mixed religions. Some parents from other countries send their children there. In spite of this diversity, the parents were generally in agreement about rules and were consistent in their opinions and attitudes.

Trinity students, like many urban youngsters, are given a reasonable amount of freedom of movement, according to the survey. By the time they are eight or nine, most of them use public transportation and run errands unaccompanied. But parents agreed that they expected their sons and daughters to keep them informed of their whereabouts. *All* the par-

RESULTS OF PARENTS ASSOCIATION QUESTIONNAIRE*

| Grade | K | 1 | 2 | 3 | 4 | 5 | 6 | 7 | 8 | 9 | 10 | 11 | 12 |
|---|---|---|---|---|---|---|---|---|---|---|---|---|---|
| No. in grade | 44 | 46 | 44 | 42 | 46 | 53 | 55 | 60 | 57 | 109 | 96 | 88 | 82 |
| No. of responses | 27 | 37 | 19 | 24 | 33 | 38 | 27 | 29 | 28 | 50 | 50 | 46 | 18 |
| Percent of responses | 61% | 80% | 43% | 57% | 72% | 72% | 49% | 48% | 49% | 46% | 52% | 52% | 20% |
| Mothers work full-time | 56% | 46% | 37% | 58% | 45% | 55% | 67% | 45% | 32% | 46% | 48% | 48% | 61% |
| Mothers work part-time | 22% | 35% | 32% | 17% | 15% | 18% | 7% | 31% | 36% | 26% | 20% | 20% | 17% |
| Parents married | All | 86% | 68% | 88% | 79% | 71% | 56% | 66% | 68% | 68% | 64% | 67% | 61% |
| *Freedom of Movement* | | | | | | | | | | | | | |
| Use of elevators | Own Bldg. 67% | 60% | 64% | 73% | 78% | 87% | 93% | All | All | All | All | All | All |
| Go to and from school alone | 0 | Only 1 | 0 | 33% | 64% | 95% | 96% | All | 96% | All | All | All | All |
| Play on sidewalk | 22% | 24% | 63% | 71% | 76% | 87% | 89% | 97% | 93% | All | All | All | All |
| Run neighborhood errands | 0 | 8% | 22% | 58% | 88% | 92% | 89% | 97% | 93% | All | All | All | All |
| Go to local park alone | 0 | 0 | 10% | 25% | 52% | 55% | 59% | 83% | 93% | G—77% B—93% | G—85% B—All | G—All B—88% | G—All B—All |
| Attend neighborhood movies | 0 | 0 | 0 | 13% | 18% | 55% | 59% | 86% | 96% | G—91% B—93% | G—95% B—All | G—All B—All | G—All B—All |
| Go to department stores | 0 | 0 | 0 | 0 | 0 | 8% | 22% | 34% | 54% | G—86% B—93% | G—All B—90% | G—95% B—96% | G—All B—All |

| | | | | | | | | | | | | | |
|---|---|---|---|---|---|---|---|---|---|---|---|---|---|
| Go to pinball or video centers | 0 | 0 | Only 1 | 0 | 15% | 26% | 19% | 38% | 43% | G—27% B—46% | G—50% B—67% | G—45% B—69% | G—70% B—63% |
| Attend movies in Times Square | 0 | 0 | 0 | 0 | 0 | 0 | 0 | 0 | 0 | G—9% B—36% | G—30% B—27% | G—50% B—35% | G—60% B—75% |
| Attend rock concerts | 0 | 0 | 0 | 0 | 0 | Only 1 | Only 1 | Only 1 | 14% | G—41% B—57% | G—70% B—73% | G—85% B—92% | G—All B—All |
| Stay alone during day | 1 hr. 10% | 14% | 16% | 50% | 76% | 89% | All | All | 96% | All | All | All | All |
| Stay alone during evening | 0 | 0 | 0 | Only 1 | 27% | 71% | 81% | 90% | 79% | G—91% B—All | G—All B—All | G—All B—All | G—All B—All |
| Stay alone overnight | 0 | 0 | 0 | 0 | Only 1 | 0 | 0 | Only 1 | 11% | G—18% B—32% | G—50% B—37% | G—65% B—81% | G—90% B—All |
| Stay alone for weekend | 0 | 0 | 0 | 0 | Only 1 | 0 | 0 | 0 | 0 | Only G—1 B—25% | G—15% B—27% | G—40% B—54% | G—90% B—All |
| Ride bike in the park | 0 | 0 | Only 1 | 0 | 21% | 18% | 15% | 52% | 46% | G—36% B—39% | G—40% B—60% | G—45% B—62% | G—80% B—67% |
| Ride bike alone in the street | 0 | 0 | 0 | 4% | 15% | 29% | 15% | 45% | 32% | G—45% B—46% | G—45% B—83% | G—50% B—81% | G—80% B—83% |
| Ride bike to school | 0 | 0 | Only 1 | Only 1 | 6% | Only 1 | 0 | 24% | 21% | G—14% B—32% | G—35% B—53% | G—40% B—65% | G—80% B—83% |
| Ride bus alone | 0 | 0 | 29% | 39% | 84% | 85% | 79% | 93% | All | All | All | All | All |

Below 7th grade, days only—Above 7th, most had some time restrictions when alone.

| | | | | | | | | | | | | |
|---|---|---|---|---|---|---|---|---|---|---|---|---|
| Ride taxi alone | G—All B—All | G—95% B—All | G—95% B—All | G—86% B—90% | 75% | 69% | 59% | 21% | 4% | 0 | 0 | 0 |
| Ride subway alone | G—90% B—88% | G—60% B—85% | G—55% B—77% | G—50% B—57% | 54% | 14% | Only 1 | Only 1 | 0 | 0 | 0 | 0 |
| Parents discussed muggings and sexual advances | All | 96% | 96% | 88% | 96% | 83% | All | 89% | 94% | 79% | 63% | 46% |
| Have curfews | G—50% B—88% | G—75% B—81% | G—90% B—80% | G—91% B—72% | All | All | All | All | All | NA | NA | NA |
| Most frequent curfew weekday | G—11:30 B—10:30 | G—10 B—8 | G—10/11 B—9/11 | G&B 10:00 | 6:00 | 6:00 | 6:00 6:30 | By Dark | By Dark | NA | NA | NA |
| weekend | G—2AM B—1AM | G—2AM B—12:30 | G—12 B—12/1 | G&B 11/12 | 9:00 10:00 | 6:00 9:00 | 6:00 9:30 | By Dark | By Dark | NA | NA | NA |
| Must go directly home after school | 0 | 11% | 34% | 34% | 32% | 48% | 81% | 63% | All | NA | NA | NA |
| Change destination—must consult first | 33% | 59% | 74% | 78% | 64% | 69% | All | 92% | All | NA | NA | NA |
| Sleep over during week | 67% | 33% | 18% | 34% | 21% | 14% | 19% | 21% | Only 1 | 4% | 16% | 5% |

Ride subway alone notes: Below 5th grade, days only. Days only grades 5—10: Time restrictions grades 11 and 12.

*Trinity School Parents Association, 1982

ents of students in the fourth through eighth grades who answered the questionnaire had set curfews for their children. For the younger groups, the time was "when it got dark or at 6:00 P.M."

The majority of students in grades five through twelve, the survey showed, were given a comfortable amount of freedom to decide what to do, but they were expected to communicate frequently with their parents. Changes in plans or destinations were expected to be discussed.

One question Trinity parents were asked was, "Have you discussed with your child the specific dangers he or she might encounter, especially muggings and sexual advances?" Virtually all parents who responded had talked about personal safety at home with their children, even though they knew the school offered some instruction. The older the children, the greater the number of parents who talked about safety. As for the younger children in kindergarten and first grade, only 33 percent and 46 percent of the parents discussed these subjects. For the second grade it was 63 percent; third grade, 79 percent; fourth grade, 94 percent; fifth grade, 89 percent; sixth grade, all; seventh grade, 83 percent; eighth grade, 96 percent; ninth grade, 88 percent; tenth grade, 96 percent; eleventh grade, 96 percent; and twelfth grade, all.

The following list of questions about children's independent activities was adapted from the questionnaire sent to the Trinity School parents. If your child is still too young to go out alone, these questions can help you think through a schedule of what activities are appropriate for different ages. If your child is already partially independent and you are wondering about the next step, the activities below may suggest gradual ways of increasing his or her independence. The answers of the Trinity parents are included in the preceding pages.

## Questions to Ask Yourself

1. Which of the following do you allow your child to do when unaccompanied by an adult?

- Go to and from school.
- Play on the sidewalk in front of your house or in the yard.
- Do neighborhood errands.
- Go to the local park.
- Walk the dog.
- Ride the bus.
- Attend movies in the neighborhood.
- Attend rock concerts.
- Go to downtown department stores.
- Attend movies out of the neighborhood.
- Go to video game centers.
- Stay alone at home during the day.
- Stay alone at home during the evening.
- Stay alone at home overnight.
- Stay alone at home for a weekend.
- Ride bike to school.
- Ride bike in the park.
- Ride bike in the streets.

2. Do you require that your child consult you before going out? Before changes in destination or plans?
3. Have you got a curfew time for your child?
4. If your child travels to and from school alone, is he or she required to go directly home after school? If not, may he or she study at a friend's house? Must the child notify you upon arrival elsewhere?

It is always interesting to see how much responsibility children are given under a variety of circumstances, even if you live in a very different type of community. The safety arrangements of other parents can help you formulate your own. They can point up some things that may not have occurred to you and enable you to plan in advance how you want to handle them.

The best protection for children lies in their knowing potential dangers and preparing to avoid them. Although difficult, it is necessary to tell your child what things are unsafe and what to do to cope with them, without dwelling on the dangers in any detail. Just answer a child's questions. Talk about what to do in certain situations; let the child learn there are competent and calm ways to act.

Since you cannot physically be with your children all the time as they get older, giving them knowledge and self-assurance will be the best protection you can provide. Informed children will be better able to protect themselves. (Specific suggestions for different kinds of situations will be offered later in this book.)

Encourage your child to talk to you freely about his or her fears and concerns, and particularly about any bad experiences. Take them seriously, no matter how trivial they might at first appear to you.

Good family communication is the foundation of personal safety. Establish this communication first, and the rules will flow more easily. You will be understood and listened to more readily. Then you will be doing all you can to help your child be safe in an unsafe world.

# ◾ 3 ◾

# Teach Your Children Well—And Early

AT the dinner table, a first grader, obviously impressed, was telling the safety lessons he had learned from a police officer who had come to school that day. His four-year-old brother listened with rapt attention to the instructions about how to handle strangers. Their mother was afraid that the younger boy might become fearful at hearing about all the things a stranger might be planning to harm a child. After dinner, she asked him what he had learned. "If a stranger comes up and offers you candy," the four-year-old told her, "you grab the candy and run."

There is probably no parent living who has not told a child not to take candy from a stranger or "Don't ever get into a car with a stranger." Most parents begin their safety training with warnings about strangers. But contrary to popular opinion, this is far from the perfect opening.

Experts point out that many young children are uncertain about the meaning of the word—and concept—of "stranger." A better beginning, therefore, is to ask your child what a stranger is. The answers you get may surprise you.

Some young children confuse the idea of a stranger with a monster or a person wearing a mask or a television cartoon "bad" person or someone who looks unfriendly. Children often assume that a bad person will be easily identifiable by looking bad in the way that the bad guys in the old Westerns always wore black hats. So your first task is to make sure they really understand what a stranger is.

Teach your children that the word "stranger" means *any* person they do not know. A parent should also explain that a bad stranger who could hurt them will often appear friendly; children often mistakenly assume that a bad person will jump out of the bushes and snarl at them.

Learning to distinguish friend from stranger does not have to mean that children lose faith in people. They grow up in a circle of trusted members of the family, neighbors and friends. In time the circle grows larger and includes teachers, bus drivers, clerks in neighborhood shops and others. But even a young child has to learn that the trusted circle does not include everyone.

As children grow older, they learn about strangers. A two-year-old will touch the arm of another passenger in a crowded bus and play with almost anyone who smiles at him. A five-year-old with her mother, seeing a strange-looking man in a parking lot, will merely stare. Once they are safely past, a mother can say, "I know that man looked weird, but you should not stop and stare at people." Gradually, a child learns which situations to avoid and how to avoid them.

To alert children to the idea that some people might harm them can be painful for parents. "Jack is such a trusting and open child," a mother says about her four-year-old. "I want him to keep his beautiful world. He believes that everyone is a friend. I don't want him becoming suspicious or fearful."

But that is not the only way. Telling a child that some bad

people do exist is very different from telling them that the world is a bad place, full of bad people. You must balance your admonitions with some positive statements, even such simple ones as "Most people are good, but there are a few who are not" and "When we don't know people, we don't know if they are good or bad." Generally, children will take their cues and their view of the world from your actions. If you are generally open and friendly—but appropriately cautious—they will follow your lead.

After you are sure a child knows what a stranger is, go on to discuss the different lures or bribes that can be used and how they should not be accepted. Tell children that to get their attention and confidence strangers will more often try sweets and sweet talk than threats and violence. Your cautions against taking any money, offers to see pets, go on rides, etc. will have more meaning to a child when offered in this context.

It is disturbing to report that in a California study, six- to nine-year-olds gave the "wrong" answers to questions concerning how to handle an offer from a stranger in over half the situations they were asked about. (See Chapter 8.) Quite naturally, offers of some pleasant activity or attractive gifts are tempting to young children.

Teach your child the correct response to offers from strangers, but do it over time. Do not expect a child to remember the warning not to take candy from strangers after being told only once or twice. What is the child's best response to such an offer? He should ignore it and walk away quickly. If the adult making the offer is in a car, the child should walk away in the opposite direction from the way the car is headed.

## Be Realistic Without Being Scary

No matter how young a child is, it is important to put your warnings in the context of competence, e.g., "This is what we can do to deal with a dangerous situation," so that, under your guidance, they develop confidence, along with the necessary caution. You are teaching them to be conscious of the potential hazards and to take certain precautions not to frighten them, but to protect their own safety.

This chapter deals with children from preschool age through the early elementary school grades, roughly from ages four to eight. By the age of eight, many children will be ready to go to school and visit friends by themselves, but some will not be. This does not mean that they are backward or immature. In some cases they may face more difficult situations on the streets where they live or where their school is located. Parents must assess their particular situation and make a decision based not just on what other children do at the same age but on the basis of their own realities.

For example, in New York City, Detective Jack Meeks of the Police Department's Crime Prevention Section says that children in early elementary grades should be accompanied to and from school by a parent, another responsible adult or an older child. He feels that warnings alone are not sufficient protection for big-city school children in the early grades. For children living in the suburbs who may only have to walk a short block to a school bus, things are obviously more relaxed.

Safety rules will vary with the circumstances, communities and, of course, the ages of the children involved. But what matters most for all children is to help them develop a sixth sense which enables them to avoid danger. Like an adult, a child needs to be able to spot situations that can lead to trouble.

Younger children must be taught what to do and how to

handle certain situations *before* they actually face them. The worst way to deal with the problem is to begin issuing safety instructions the night before a child will go to school alone for the first time. Preparations should start gradually, by showing them which places to avoid along the way, how to cross the street and where to go for help if necessary.

As you start to talk about safety, you may find that a child of about five or six may have many fantasies about his or her strength. When you bring up the question of how a child might react to a physical threat, you may get an answer such as "I'd smash him" or "I'd give him a karate chop." Often these childish responses are playbacks of what they have seen on television.

Children frequently exhibit a lot of bravado. Dreams of being all-powerful hide feelings of helplessness. Don't scold, ridicule or put down these imaginary feats of derring-do; correct them gently. Say something simple but straightforward: "You aren't big and strong enough yet to win out over an adult." The idea that a small child can take on an adult or a much bigger child should be firmly discouraged, but without destroying a child's sense of confidence. You can stress that there are ways children, too, can be useful. For example, they can be witnesses or seek adult help when they see another child being hurt or bullied.

If you are with young children and are unfortunate enough to witness an unpleasant incident, the example of your own response will be the best teacher. Your child will learn more from what you do and how you handle the incident than from anything you may say. You can follow the example of *Parents* magazine editor-in-chief Elizabeth Crow. She and her children witnessed a mugging at gunpoint. Afterwards she and her husband made a special effort to emphasize to their children how responsive the police had been. They also pointed out that the crime, while frightening and serious, had been the only such incident they had ever encountered in

their neighborhood. It would have been easy, in the heat of
the moment, to magnify the incident into an overwhelming
illustration of the horrors of a frightening world—clearly not
in the children's best interests. Being realistic about the world
does not justify blowing up one bad experience in a way that
could easily color a child's entire view of the world.

## Being a Prudent Parent

Establish family safety policies when your children are
young. For example, being able to go out to play alone at a
friend's house down the street or going to school without
adult supervision are not unconditional privileges. You always make it clear where the boundaries are. Young children are not permitted to come home after dark or cross a
busy intersection alone. The principle of gradualness must
be started at an early age.

There are some sections where even to go to a neighbor's
house or a local candy store calls for the company at least of
a child's older brother or sister. This is sadly enough the
case in many inner-city neighborhoods. One black woman,
who has six children, told me: "My kids know they have to
wait till they are bigger to go out alone on the streets. They
always wait for me or someone older to take them. I don't
like it and they don't like it, but that's the way it is. We keep
trouble away from us this way."

Be specific in your instructions. Vagueness confuses and
even frightens a child, and makes it harder to know how to
behave. Think through what you consider appropriate, and
then lay it out carefully. For example, "You can go to play
with Susie because she lives on the same side of the street
and you don't have to cross," or "You may cross the street
in front of the house, but not the intersection at the next
block." Your instructions are more likely to be followed if

they are spelled out precisely. You make it very clear in specific examples what being allowed to go out alone means and does not mean.

A vital goal of your family safety sessions is to foster and develop your children's basic instincts of self-preservation. You want to teach them to develop respect for their own "funny feelings" or hunches about people and situations. Such instincts are among their best protection.

What complicates matters is that children are naturally taught to obey adults—that is what "good" children do. In a sense, they have to unlearn some earlier training in order to protect themselves adequately. It is important to make sure that a child is also allowed to develop the capacity—under the proper circumstances—to say, "No, I don't want to." Many children have been victimized because they were afraid to say NO to an adult.

## What Should Young Children Be Learning?

1. Not to wander off alone.
2. Never to go anywhere with a stranger.
3. Never to run into the street.
4. Always to ask mother, father or adult guardian before they go off with a known person.
5. Their addresses and phone numbers.
6. Respect for police, school crossing guards, etc.

Although it may seem convenient to bring up a compliant child, in the long run, safety may depend on your child's ability to act quickly on a "funny feeling" or a generally negative vibration to a particular adult or situation.

A child should be allowed to say he does not like a particular person or place and be able, at home, to voice likes and dislikes freely. If a child does not want Uncle Harry to kiss her, those wishes should be respected.

Children should also learn how to say no in any potentially exploitative situation, even with their friends. Part of feeling safe is developing a strong sense of self. For a young child, this may include saying no to a friend who may want to borrow a new sweater. Parents often make the mistake of thinking that children must be unquestioningly generous with their possessions. For example, if Jane gets a new sweater for Christmas, her friend Susie may want to borrow it. Jane needs to have learned from her parents that it is all right to say no to Susie, even though Susie may be her best friend. Since the sweater is brand-new and Jane has not worn it yet, it is natural not to feel like lending it. Parents can help by making it clear that Jane did the right thing. Susie need not be angry or hurt. Jane can let her friend know that she still likes her and perhaps offer to lend her another sweater.

The point is that this form of communication is as important to children's sense of competence and self-esteem as practicing yelling or telling someone who is bothering them, ''Leave me alone.'' A child begins to gain confidence from practice in situations which foster a feeling of success with coping in general as well as in circumstances that are safety-related.

At this time in your child's life, you will be developing your own parenting style and part of this is your approach to safety. Don't worry if you cannot always sound as cheerful and confident as you think an ideal parent should. The ideal parent does not exist. There is nothing wrong if your child senses your concern. You need not be perfect to give your child the necessary safety education. Be yourself. If it relaxes you to ''prepare'' what you are going to say, do so. Talk to your spouse or friends who are parents. They may often contribute sound ideas on how to present difficult topics. The parents of children just a little older than yours can usually offer useful suggestions based on experience.

You may wish to meet with your child's teacher or get a PTA group to devote an evening to a safety program. Ideas that work well for one family may help others, and many parents in your neighborhood will be glad you started an organized interest in safety. Your community may be stimulated to develop what some neighborhoods have already begun—a program of "helping hand" or "safe haven" houses, clearly marked homes to which children may safely go in times of emergency.

One of the best ways to teach children what they should do in a given situation when they are without adults is to play "What if" games or tell stories which demonstrate what children can do for themselves. You can begin by trying something such as, "What if you were in the street and someone asked you to come to their house and see their new kittens?" Don't be alarmed if a child gives the "wrong" answer at first. How much better to give the wrong answer to you at home than in a real situation! You have plenty of time to teach the way you want them to behave.

The game or story format is good for many reasons. It means that personal safety talks are offered in a natural setting. It offers an opportunity to make clear that you want to know what is bothering a child, no matter what the circumstances. It provides a favorable context for communication about potentially awkward subjects.

Once begun, you can introduce many subjects from "What if we are separated in a department store?" to "What if something happened and you were afraid to tell me?" These games encourage youngsters to think for themselves. Knowing what you want them to do under certain conditions gives them confidence in their ability to take care of themselves.

There is an added bonus: games are an interesting way to find out what your child already knows, and what needs to be learned. It may also provide some insights into fears your child may find it hard to express directly.

With younger children, your directions and explanations

should always be simple. Remember the story about the boy who came home from school and asked, "Where do I come from?" His parents, thinking him very precocious, gave him a complete talk about the sexual facts of life. When they had finished, he looked very confused and told them, "I wanted to know where I came from. My friend Johnny comes from St. Louis."

## Some "What if" Questions for Younger Children

1. We are separated in a shopping center, in the movies, at the beach?
2. You are lost in a department store, in the park, at a parade?
3. A stranger offered you candy or presents to leave the playground?
4. A stranger wanted you to get into his car?
5. A stranger started fussing with your clothing?
6. Your friends wanted to play with matches?
7. Someone you did not know asked your name and phone number?

Closer to home, my husband remembers walking home from a museum with one of our sons, then age eight, and explaining some of the exhibits they had just seen. "Daddy," our son said, obviously bored by the explanation he did not understand, "Please tell me about it when I'm older."

## Going Out Alone

How do you tell when your child is "ready" to cross a street or go to school without adult supervision? It can be a big step. For younger children, the trip to and from school will probably be their first time out alone.

One of the surest signs is that the child feels ready. Your child will prod you repeatedly. (A one-time request does not mean much more than that your child is thinking about it.) While a child's wishes should not be taken as the last word, they should be listened to seriously. By the same token, a youngster who seems reluctant should never be forced to go alone. There are probably good reasons for the doubts, even if he or she cannot articulate them.

On the other hand, if all the other children in your area are allowed to cross the street alone and yours is not, he or she is likely to feel like a baby. In this case, it is important to check with the parents of friends and classmates. This is a time when you want to take into account what other parents and children are doing. You also want to find out what other children will be walking to school or the bus stop with yours.

Do not expect this to be an easy decision. It is perfectly natural for you to have a few doubts, whichever side you finally choose. Make the process of gaining independence gradual and specific. The checklist below should help you clarify your thoughts.

### Is Your Child Ready to Go to School Alone?

1. Does the child want to?
2. Are there other children from the class or neighborhood to walk with?
3. Does your child know his or her address and phone number?
4. Can your child phone mommy and daddy at work? Are those numbers known?
5. Does your child know how to contact another adult if anyone is needed?
6. Have you practiced going over the route your child will use?

7. Does your child know your family safety rules?
8. Does your child cross the streets involved safely and easily?
9. Does your child know where to go if help is needed?
10. Have you pointed out any danger spots—a bad crossing or a deserted house—on the way to school?

I am assuming that you have gone over the route to school, have walked it with your child and along the way have pointed out important things. In particular, you have told your children that if they are walking home near dusk, they should stay away from doorways, shrubs and large trees. (If there are no sidewalks in your neighborhood, you have demonstrated—not just explained—that a child should walk on the side of the street facing traffic. In this situation, it would probably be advisable to wait until the child is a little older than if there are sidewalks and a well-defined place to walk.)

## Changes in Plans

Find out your school's policy for children leaving the building at the end of the day. Many schools have established procedures for responding to a request that a child be released to the custody of an adult other than the known parent or guardian. Today's increasingly common problem of kidnapping in child-custody disputes poses relatively new but troublesome safety problems for families and schools. Be sure to leave clear instructions that identify exactly who may collect your child after school.

In some places children are allowed to leave only in the way they arrived (on the bus, walking), prescribed by the parent at the beginning of the year. If your school has no set procedure, you will want to make your particular wishes clear. In addition, you may want to join others in formulating a policy with specific guidelines.

You will, of course, have taught your children that it is family policy never to allow themselves to be picked up by a stranger. When asked the question, "*What if* an adult you did not know told you 'Your mother said I should take you home?','' the right answer is "My mother wouldn't do that" or "My mother wouldn't say that without telling me first." (It is difficult for most children to say "I don't believe you" to an adult, even if they don't.)

Part of training children to go to and from school alone is teaching them to let you know if there are any changes in plans. Your child should already have been developing this habit because you or the baby-sitter have always called when there was a change of plan, or if homecoming was later than expected. When something happens to disrupt things, no matter how innocent, it can be a bad moment for parents.

I still remember one afternoon some years ago at about 3:30 when our baby-sitter interrupted an interview I was doing for a rushed article. "I met the school bus, but John wasn't on it. I thought I'd better tell you."

I felt a rush of panic, but told myself not to be alarmed. "Did you call the school? Maybe he missed the bus."

"I did. The teacher was not there. The secretary told me there was no one left waiting."

I tried to keep my voice steady, even though I felt anxiety welling up. "Call the bus service. The number is on the list next to the phone. The regular driver knows John and he might remember whether he got off with a friend."

For the next few minutes, I could barely concentrate on my work. Fortunately, we had just about finished when the baby-sitter came in. My fears grew stronger. Thoughts of kidnappings, sexual molestation and murder raced through my mind. I tried to tell myself to be calm and sensible. There must be some perfectly reasonable explanation.

After a few more minutes which seemed like hours, John came home. He had got a ride with his friend's mother and she had to stop for an errand. My relief was tempered by my anger.

"Why didn't you call us? You know I have told you always to do that. Do you know how frightened I was when I heard you were not on the bus. Don't ever do it again."

"I'm sorry," he said. "I thought I'd get home at the same time as the bus and it wouldn't matter."

I snapped at him. "We'll talk about it later." Then I began to feel a little guilty for talking like that. Why did I get so upset? I realized I had probably scared him. But it is easy to panic when you don't know where a child is. It does not matter whether you live in a busy city or a quiet suburb. Each place and each parent has his or her own visions of particular horrors. We do not want to burden our children with them, but we have to teach them not to worry us unnecessarily. It is important for them to learn to let you know about a change in plans, even if very ordinary, or to notify you when they know they will be home later than usual. A few minutes either way does not count, but a half hour or more does.

### School Bus Checklist*

*For Parents:*
1. Know the route your child walks to the bus stop. Go over it before school starts. A child should feel comfortable knowing the area. At the beginning of the school year, if it is the first time alone, you

*Adapted from the U.S. Department of Transportation, National Highway Traffic Safety Administration.

may want to walk your child or find someone older
to go along.

2. Help your child to learn his or her school-bus driver's name.
3. Help your child to be ready early enough to arrive
   at the bus stop on time.

*For Children:*

1. Enter the bus single file, with no crowding or
   pushing. Always use the handrail.
2. Do not keep feet, lunch box, books or anything
   else in the aisle. It should be clear.
3. Sit down right away.
4. Stay seated while the bus is moving.
5. Keep hands, arms, legs and head inside bus.
6. Keep windows closed, unless you have permission
   to open them.
7. Never throw anything in the bus or out of the window.
8. Stand up and get ready to leave only when the bus
   comes to a complete stop.
9. When you leave a school bus, look both ways before crossing the street or highway.

## Where Can They Go for Help?

You can help children deal with many difficult situations
as they gain independence if you let them know that there
are people on whom they can call if they think they are in
trouble. The first and most obvious group includes not only
the immediate family, but also aunts, uncles, grandparents,
cousins and some friends who are very close to the family.
Children need to be told explicitly that it is natural for prob-

lems to arise at times, which they cannot be expected to solve by themselves. Getting outside help from adults they know and trust is the sensible course and is in no way babyish; in fact, it is a grown-up thing to do. You can tell them that adults often turn to others for help, too.

In addition to family and friends, you want to point out helpful people in the community. Again, at first these should be people the children know and who know them. And, of course, they should not be afraid to turn to a policeman if they are lost or have other problems. This is why it is important for your children to get a positive image of the police at an early age. Perhaps you can take the time to meet some officers and have your children talk to them. In addition, you can take the opportunity when you are out to identify people who will be helpful, such as park attendants, movie theater ushers and museum and shopping center security guards.

The fact that you are pointing out some strangers who can help children means that you are not training them to be distrustful of people at all times. Your goal is to help develop judgment, which of course is a lifelong process. But the foundations you build in early childhood are vital.

Parents need to take some time to think about the potential dangers a child may encounter; that is the first step in teaching personal safety. Thinking over what to do in an emergency while still safe at home leads to better decisions. If you have given your instructions beforehand, children will not have to figure out frantically what to do under the stress of an actual encounter. It is almost impossible to think clearly when fear and panic are present.

Advance planning will alert youngsters to potential dangers so they are better able to avoid them. This is one way you can reassure your children they have some control in coping with whatever street problems they may face. They will have learned the best ways to deal with any situations that may arise.

# ◼ 4 ◼

# Learning to Be
# Street Smart

"**B**ASICALLY, there are two types of kids, those who
have street smarts and those who don't," says Ed Muir,
head of School Safety for the United Federation of Teachers
in New York. "The ones who have it pick up techniques
from other kids and older siblings, who tell them things such
as 'Don't go on that block' or 'This is a safe street.' And
their parents have helped them learn how to protect themselves."

In order to do this, parents must acknowledge the realities
of urban life. "Many middle-class kids are not street
smart," Muir says. "Their parents wrap them in a protective cocoon. They are insulated and lack contact with the
street scene. They spend more time in the company of adults
than with other, street-wise children. When they have to
travel out of their neighborhoods in late middle school at
about age 11 or in high school, they are in trouble." Children who have been overprotected frequently feel they are
free to do anything they want. But once on the streets, they
quickly find out this is no longer possible.

Another problem is that some children look "muggable," as one boy put it, when talking about a classmate. The term is hard to define and not easy to pin down. It can be applied to children who daydream on the streets, who are preoccupied, or those who are "line counters," as one policeman called it. Sometimes it means a youngster does not look alert or well-coordinated when walking. Boys and girls can frequently sense it about each other. One element that my informant was able to cite was that his muggable friend "looked rich," which meant he wore blazers and shoes rather than sweaters and sneakers, and he usually sported a wristwatch.

Ed Muir agrees that there is such a thing as looking like an easy mark. "It is an intangible. But one part that can be controlled is dress and appearance. A well-groomed kid in status jeans and brand-name sneakers with an expensive book bag is looking for trouble. A child should wear a plain shirt and simple jeans. He should not stand out in any way."

Most parents are not overprotective or insensitive to appearance, even though they may be worried. They do prepare their children gradually for independence, giving them the freedom they need—within limits. Muir is a case in point. He has a teenage son whose job involves working at night. Sometimes he has to come home after 10 o'clock. Muir calls for his son and drives him home because he does not consider it safe for anyone to take the New York subway late at night.

What do we mean when we say that children are street smart? Generally, it means they are skilled in handling themselves in whatever situations they encounter outside their homes. They have become able to deal with the dangers in their immediate environment. Although we may be reluctant, we must acknowledge that this is a positive achievement. If children are going to live in a dangerous world, they had better learn how to cope.

## Street Safety Rules

1. Walk to and from school with a group of friends.
2. Don't linger in the schoolyard when the rest of your friends have left.
3. Know your school route.
4. If you have any problem after school, go back to find a teacher when there is no one at home.
5. Walk in the middle of the sidewalk; avoid bushes and doorways.
6. Know your neighborhood. Remember safe places to go if you need immediate help—storekeepers, gas stations, a nearby friend, local fire and police stations, the post office.
7. Know the location of public phone booths in your area.
8. Never flash money, bus passes, transistor radios, cameras or other possessions. Don't tell your classmates you don't know well about the things you have in your locker or at home.

Street-wise children know how to use their eyes and other senses to perceive what is happening around them to avoid being caught like flies in a spider web. If there is an unruly group of bigger guys down on the right-hand corner, they know it's smart to cross the street. If there are just one or two kids who do not look tough and plenty of people walking up and down the street, then they know that no evasive action is necessary. They know the difference.

We all wish it were possible for children not to have to be street smart. We realize sadly that they cannot remain as innocent as we would like and still be safe on the streets. Once children move about on their own, they must be prepared to face some possible unpleasantness—threats, tauntings and, of course, muggings.

The word "mugging" covers many different situations. It is not a precise term. When children report having been mugged, it may mean anything from an ugly incident, such as older kids blocking their way, saying, "Hey, asshole!" to a full-scale encounter with someone demanding their possessions at knifepoint.

By definition, a mugger takes you by surprise; he comes up from behind or out of a doorway. There are often two or three against one. Muggers are not looking for a fair fight. They are looking for an easy victory. This is why children and the elderly are at special risk. The typical mugger does not attack a six-foot two-inch 190-pound male walking down the street in bright daylight; the odds are not good in that situation. Muggers look for a weaker individual who is vulnerable and unprotected. They do not abide by any rules. They want to take advantage in any way possible.

Being mugged is always a personal confrontation. Sometimes, one boy told me, the threat of physical harm is not even mentioned, it is implied. Frequently, no weapon is visible. When the mugger is older and bigger than the victim, a simple demand in a menacing voice is usually enough.

When children were asked by New York Parents League safety trainers under what conditions if thus confronted, they would surrender their bikes, nearly all replied, "When the mugger is your size or bigger." This is the same criterion most adults would use in a similar situation.

New York City Detective Jack Meeks explains that officially the police do not acknowledge the word "mugging." "We don't use the term," he says. "We call it a robbery." But in popular talk, the word "mugging" continues to be used for any unpleasant confrontation in which there is at least the implied threat of bodily harm. "Think of it this way," my son said when we discussed the matter. "They can't mug a grocery store or a bank. They can only mug a person."

For many urban children, being mugged is almost a rite of passage. Elementary school younsters often ask each other, "Have you been mugged yet?" Second and third graders, even if they themselves have not yet gone out alone, often know someone who has been mugged and can tell about the experience secondhand.

Although not entirely conclusive, available evidence suggests that boys report more such experiences than girls. Ed Muir reports that in some sections of New York, there are gangs of girls that attack girls. But most observers agree that boys are more likely to be mugged than girls.

In New York City, where personal safety is discussed more frequently than in most other places, many boys consider it "macho" to be mugged by roaming boys from different ethnic groups. Afterward, the confrontation is frequently embellished in the same way that men in the past added flavor to war exploits told long after the events.

The macho image, and the problems it poses for boys, are very real and needs to be addressed. Some grown men have never come to terms with their own feelings about the matter, and the idea of ever giving way to any threat seems so damaging to their masculine image that they will risk being killed for an endangered wallet or even a speeding ticket.

A New York boy who has been mugged, by his count, half a dozen times reports that he was never hurt and was only afraid on one occasion, when a boy showed him a gun which may or may not have been real. The mugging routine, he said, was predictable. "Usually what happened was that a group of black or Hispanic youths surrounded me and asked for the time or a quarter. I responded that I didn't have a watch or that I was broke. After a few moments of small talk, they finally came out with 'Give us your money or bus pass.' My final response was to partly submit. That is, I would give them either some of my money or my bus pass. Never everything.

"Why? Because, while I seldom felt fear or the threat of physical injury, another feeling had to be fought during the mugging: humiliation. It was awful to come home and admit that I had been stupid enough to keep all my money in one pocket, or that my bus pass had a five-dollar bill next to it. If I could get away with only satisfying the muggers' demands partially, I would prove my chutzpah, my cleverness and my street sense.

"Humiliation was the thing I most fought during the muggings. If I could tell my friends about the money they didn't get, whether hidden in a sock, a shoe or my underwear, the harm of the mugging was minimized. All together, I must have lost five or ten dollars, three or four bus passes and a basketball. But think of all the booty they never got. That might be a funny way of looking at things, but I saved face without getting hurt."

It is important for parents not to minimize or belittle the sense of humiliation boys feel. One thing you can tell a boy whose sense of masculinity has been assailed is that he is mistaking the outer trappings of manliness for the real thing. What is he going to prove by fighting someone who may have a knife? Is he going to make his stand on some street corner now or in some arena he chooses later in life? Since the muggers are not fighting fair, it is no disgrace to give in. It is not like running away from a fair fight. You recognize that you are caught in an unequal situation. You are not "losing" because the concept of "win or lose" does not really apply. You may also want to point out that some of the stories his friends tell about their mugging experiences may be exaggerated. Tell him about your own experiences with your friends' stories to support this.

Give your child the advantage of your perspective, pointing out that the mugger's behavior is irrational and unpredictable. In this context, stress that he is not a timid loser by giving up his possessions to a mugger. Of course, a youngster will still feel terrible. Who wouldn't? But if you can get your children to look at being mugged as a crazy, irrational and ridiculous situation, they will find it easier to deal with.

## Street Safety Rules

1. Always tell your parents where you are going and when you will be home.
2. Do not take shortcuts through deserted areas, alleyways, vacant lots or abandoned buildings.
3. Stay alert. Be aware of your surroundings.
4. If you are asked directions from someone in a car, keep a safe distance. Do *not* move closer, even if they say they can't hear you.
5. Use public rest rooms with caution. Always have someone else with you.
6. If you see an accident or a mugging, do not get involved. Call the police or ask a shopkeeper to get help. Be prepared to give an accurate description of the incident.
7. Do not go alone to movies, ball parks or amusement parks.

While more boys appear to be involved in muggings and other unpleasant incidents, girls are by no means immune. Just as boys prey mostly on other boys, girls more often attack other girls.

In Dr. Nicholas Zill's study of child victimization, in which over half the children reported being bothered by other children or adults while they were playing, both boys and girls were involved. And a slightly higher percentage of girls reported being afraid of being hurt than did the boys. (See Chapter 1.)

Unlike the past, today many parents try to train both boys

and girls to protect themselves in similar ways. But behavioral scientists report that others still engage in more rough-and-tumble play with boys. Parents and other adults are much more likely to tell a boy to fight back when picked on. A girl is still more likely to be told to walk away from the situation or to report it to a teacher or another adult.

But there is beginning to be some change. More girls now are taught how to size up situations. A few years ago, one of my son's classmates was out running with a girlfriend when they were stopped by a smaller boy who demanded money. They pushed him aside and continued running without further trouble.

A New York City mother told me about her daughter, age 12, who was attacked by several girls her own age apparently intent on beating her up and tearing her clothing rather than taking her money. The girl was able to escape by hailing a taxi that fortunately was approaching. One of her attackers tried to follow her into the cab. But the girl kept her assailant out of the taxi by kicking her in the stomach. She told her mother afterward, "I didn't think I could do anything like that to anybody, but I was so angry and frightened."

These are positive examples of girls knowing how to deal with such situations, but things do not always work out so well. Often, girls also have to hand over their possessions. The important thing is for them to learn, as boys do, to assess a situation and respond with safety uppermost in their minds.

Being alert and careful on the street does not mean that children need to become nervous or overcautious. They can learn to accept certain situations and even joke about muggings with each other and with their parents. It is reassuring to talk to children themselves. Even those who have had unpleasant experiences seem able to keep a balanced view of the world. "There are weirdos out there," one boy told me.

"After a while you learn to stay away from them." Another, who had been mugged a few months earlier, said it was "not such a big deal. I really don't think about it a whole lot. And I'm not going to stay home all the time."

Because of the nature of mugging, both parents and children have to acknowledge that it is usually the youngest and smallest children who are most at risk. Sadly, children just beginning to go to school by themselves, who are the least experienced, are the easiest prey. The child of elementary school age, six to twelve years old, is most often a target.

A mother whose three boys were mugged repeatedly while still in elementary school, told me half seriously, "Since they reached six feet, my sons have not had street problems." Unfortunately, physical size and age are major factors. Another mother told about her son who, before he was nine, was waylaid three times by older boys who took his bus pass and his money. The boy is older and wiser now. He carries his money in his shoe. Another youngster was regularly approached by three older boys who took his change and threatened him as he walked home from school until he decided to join some other children and change his route.

What is actually involved in a serious incident? The story of nine-year-old Jack is an example. He is attractive, sandy haired, with an engaging smile, but small for his age:

"On a Tuesday in February I was walking to school. After I had gone a few blocks, I began to feel that somebody was following me." Jack did not act on his gut feeling because he thought it might have been one of his classmates or older schoolmates playing. Sometimes they had games on the way to school where they would push and jump on each other.

Yet, a few minutes later, an older boy of 11 or 12, walked up and asked for money. "I said I didn't have any and kept walking down to the end of the block." When Jack got there, the older boy pulled a knife and asked for money again. "I gave him my money." The boy then forced him to walk down the block. He told Jack to keep "a straight face" and said "if I called to anyone he would get me. I thought he would stab me." After several more blocks of walking around at knifepoint, the mugger took Jack's book bag (he did not want the books) and had Jack empty the bag. He then ran off.

Jack talks about how he felt: "I was very scared after. Now I'm more careful about walking to school. And after religious school when it's dark, I wait for someone to go home with. If I have to go alone now, about every half block, I look over my shoulder. If I see the same person three times, I stop and wait till they pass." He told me, he makes more arrangements with friends now.

Safety expert Charles T. Bonaventura of New York City's Police Department comments, "During our interviews about past muggings, we usually find out that the victims had a sense that something was wrong. They were being followed or they sensed that a person they saw did not fit into the area." He advises children to act on their intuition. "If you have a feeling that something is going to happen, then it is going to happen and you should act accordingly. People often know better, but they don't act on their intuition and they become victims."

Bonaventura adds, "Attackers usually single out an individual, or they will chase a group of kids until one falls behind and surround that particular kid. This is basically what animals do—chase a group until one falls behind. We try to teach kids to stick together while going to school and playing. Attackers try to intimidate individuals."

One boy reported that when he was in fourth grade he and two friends were at the end of the class line, only a block from the school building, when four older boys cut them off from the group. These muggers concentrated on one of the others, so he remained unnoticed and could run to get help from the teacher.

Another boy, now in his teens, remembers the first time he was mugged when he was in third grade. It was the day after Halloween and he still had some trick-or-treat money: "Two older kids came up to us when we were trying to get into my friend's building. There was an older girl, who gave the directions, and a younger boy. We were on the steps. They were on bicycles. First they asked for directions. Then they asked the time, and then for change of a dollar. I was suspicious enough not to give them change."

Things then turned ugly. "They asked for money. I must have looked really tough—my friend said I did—though I was shaking and shivering. The boy who was mugging us did not like the way I looked and hit me in the face. Then they left. I felt really bad, but I did not report the incident to the police until the next day, and it was hopeless by then. There were so many suspects and a long wait at the station house."

The two boys, badly shaken, did not think of calling the police until one of their fathers urged it and went along with them. If conditions are right, going to the police can offer some satisfaction and relief to youngsters who have been mugged. But swift contact and a detailed description of the mugger are vital.

One of the questions that parents most often ask, Bonaventura reports, is about "mugging money," some extra small change a child can carry—never more than a dollar—to hand over during a confrontation. Like many parents we know, we used to give our boys a little extra change whey they went out. I had mixed feelings about this and so did some of our friends, but we had been advised it was a good idea.

Giving mugging money is different from sending your children out with more money than they need—never a good idea since it will set them up as easy marks. The question of whether a little extra is a good idea, whether it will placate a potential mugger or will save children from physical harm, as some believe, remains debatable. "Kids should only have money for lunch, or for their movie tickets," advises Detective Jack Meeks, "plus an emergency dime or two tucked away in a shoe or stock, should a phone call be necessary." There are so many factors involved in what happens during a mugging, it is impossible to give blanket advice. Carrying some money and learning how to use it is part of becoming independent.

One mother I spoke to says she does not believe in mugging money because, in her view, this conditions children to hand it over automatically, sometimes even to a smaller child. She says she has known this to happen. Children, she believes, should not be programmed to give up their possessions. Of course, if they have a chance to take some other evasive action, they should, and probably will. The question in these situations remains, What is a safe action?

"A lot of families give children mugging money," says Charles Bonaventura. "There have been cases where a kid is confronted and asked for money. He says he doesn't have any. Next thing you know, the kid gets hurt. But that doesn't always happen. And sometimes a mugger is not happy with what he receives and feels that maybe your child is holding back. There is no one way of answering this."

The police do advise handing over money or possessions if you believe your attacker will use force, and especially if there might be a weapon involved. "What we are trying to do is prevent children from getting into a position where they are going to be victims of a serious crime."

Whether a child should carry a small amount of additional money to give over to a mugger will remain an individual family's decision. But no matter what you decide, at no time should a child, especially a young child, carry more than an extra dollar, whether to give to muggers or for personal needs.

Children need to get used to always having some money with them, for lunch or snacks or carfare and phone calls. Parents should see to it that money is available. But the child should gradually assume responsibility for not forgetting it in the morning on the way to school. It is not advisable to be out alone without at least some small change.

And as a matter of course, you will have been telling your children all along that they must not flaunt any money or other possessions. If they take a public bus, they should wait until they get on to take out a bus pass or their change.

Confronted by someone who demands property by force or the threat of force, a child is as upset as an adult. Most observers agree that the mere threat of force always leaves you wondering afterward if you should have defended yourself.

Common sense, as well as the experts, urges you not to fight with anyone who is or might be armed. But such apparently submissive behavior poses difficult dilemmas, not about the action taken, but about its aftermath.

When my sons were little and went around the corner to buy candy, I told them to keep their money out of sight. I also impressed on them that if someone bigger came up and demanded money to "give it to them—and don't make a fuss."

Since then, my boys have grown taller and stronger, but my directions remain unchanged.

What is my message? Am I telling them that running away or passive resignation are appropriate responses to danger on the streets? Am I telling them that they are power-less?

Sometimes I think so, even though I know better. I do not blame my sons for disliking my advice. So do I. All of us would like to be able to relax. But it is not possible to relax and be safe.

Fortunately, there are other ways of viewing the situation. It takes as much courage to jeopardize your self-esteem by being cautious as it does to foolishly risk bodily harm, says Dr. Richard Rabkin, associate clinical professor of psychiatry at New York University. It is easier to replace a bike or a watch or money than it is to replace a limb if you have misjudged a situation.

Many children are angry at the idea of not being able to fight back. My son's friend was robbed of his bike by three boys, one of whom had a knife. Although he was angry, he knew he had no chance to fight against superior odds and therefore did not feel humiliated.

But a few years ago, in a different encounter, our son John was not so sure. An older and bigger boy asked to "borrow" his skateboard, a common tactic of muggers. John wisely gave it to him and watched the boy speed downhill and disappear around a corner. He knew he would never see either boy or skateboard again. He also knew he had done the "right" thing to give up his possession. But his sensible action was a far cry from his fantasies of what he would have wanted to do.

More recently, when a large, burly man asked to "see" his flute, John handed it over. He was resentful and agonized afterward about whether he could have run fast enough to get away. Even getting the flute back did not make him feel any better.

After the incident I wondered—as every parent must at some time—whether I had taught him the right lessons. Had

I, through my concern for his safety, undermined his self-esteem?

Most of us feel we have a right to fight for our possessions, and so do our children. The real hitch comes when we try to assess whether the fight is uneven and risky. In the end, it is a question of judgment and not at all a question of right and wrong. We should never make the mistake of teaching kids across the board that it is wrong to fight for possessions. What we teach them is to fight for their possessions as long as it is an equal fight. But not to be crazy and fight for possessions you don't have a chance of keeping because it will be dangerous for you if you do. What we are essentially teaching them is to fight back only when they have a fair chance.

"Kids know whom they can fight and whom they can't," says Edward A. Davies, chief of pediatrics at Lenox Hill Hospital in New York. "Some kids are more willing than others to get into a scrap. But the typical child will size up a situation pretty quickly and decide whether or not he wants to make an argument out of it." This observation from an experienced pediatrician is very comforting.

Dr. Davies believes we ought to teach our children that you can stick up for your possessions, "but if the odds are so much against your being successful, you've just got to face facts. And you don't fight to keep books, goggles, or even a bike or something else that isn't very important, in situations where you may be in danger."

Detective Meeks sums it up when he talks as a father as well as a policeman. "My fourteen-year-old is a six-footer now. I tell him if you see a kid with a knife in his hand who asks for your radio, give him your radio. I tell him I don't want him fooling around with someone with a knife.

"If there is no weapon, don't just hand anything over. If you do have a fight, keep in mind that just because you haven't seen a knife doesn't mean there is none. I'm not saying surrender to anyone you see. The idea is to use your head and size up the situation before you fight.''

## What if?

1. *Your mother gave you some money to buy an ice cream cone. On the way to Baskin Robbins, a bigger boy asks for money and threatens to hit you if you do not give it to him.*

If a child is walking home from school or going to a store and a bully approaches who demands money, says Police Detective Thomas Oates of the Montclair (New Jersey) Crime Prevention Unit, most children surprisingly are under the misapprehension that they should be ''macho,'' resist and attempt to fight the bully off, rather than give up the money.

''We tell them,'' Oates says, ''that is the last thing we want them to do. We tell them to do what the police instruct any adult to do when confronting a mugger. We tell them to give up what's asked for, get a good description of the suspect and report the information.''

When such crimes go unreported, says Oates and other police representatives, it encourages bullies to keep on preying on other children.

2. *You are at the bus stop. When the bus comes, you realize you don't have any money or a bus pass. The driver is not the one you know and so he will not let you ride the bus.*

This is an illustration of the advantage of traveling with friends who could have lent you money. In this case you would have to be late to school in order to go back home and get the needed money.

When this situation was tried out on a 10-year-old New York girl by her father, she replied, ''If I had no bus pass or money and the driver did not know me, I guess I'd have to walk." Her father was alarmed. Although he and his daughter had walked across Central Park together in the mornings, the idea that his daughter would consider doing it by herself upset him. He became tense when she gave the "wrong" answer. But it proved helpful in showing him what his daughter had to learn about safety. The father decided that he and his wife had been sheltering their daughter too much and wanted her to become more independent. It was clear that this was only one of many situations they had to talk about before they were all comfortable having her go out more on her own.

*3. You are sitting alone at Burger King eating your hamburger and drinking your shake when a stranger comes and sits down next to you.*

The best thing to do is ignore him. If he starts talking to you, change your seat. If he follows you, go and stay next to the cashier. Do not leave the restaurant until you can telephone for help or until the stranger has left.

If someone just sits near you and does not bother you, you can stay in the same place and finish eating. Do not start a conversation under any circumstances.

*4. You are riding on a bus and a stranger sits down beside you and begins to ask you a lot of questions that you don't want to answer.*

The best thing to do is to move to another seat if that is possible, preferably near the driver. If the bus is crowded, you can get up and blend in with the crowd. If you move to another seat and the stranger follows you, tell the bus driver "That man is bothering me." If only a few passengers are on the bus, it is a good idea to sit near the driver in the first place. Never feel obligated to answer the stranger's questions.

*5. You are waiting for the elevator in the lobby of your*

*building. When it comes up from the basement, there is a man in it you have never seen before who looks scary.*

If you feel uncomfortable for any reason about someone you see in an elevator, don't get on. You can always say, "I'm waiting for my friend" or "I'm waiting for my mother, go ahead without me." You never have to get on an elevator because it is there.

When inside the elevator, it is a good idea to stand near the control panel. Children too small to reach it or those who cannot read the numbers and signs should not be in an elevator without an adult.

If you are already in an elevator and someone gets on who talks or acts in a way that bothers you, push the button for the next floor and get off as fast as you can.

6. *You are in the park and a man walks up to you and says, "Please help me find my dog. He has disappeared and I can't find him."*

The best response, and the really safe one, would be to ignore the man and walk away. Many children find it more difficult to ignore a plea for help, particularly one connected with an animal, than they do a simple conversation or someone asking for directions or the time. But it is important for them to know that it is not safe to become helpful in this situation.

# ◼ 5 ◼

# When a Mugger Strikes

"**M**OST muggings are 'grab and run' affairs. The person just wants the cash. He doesn't want a fight. And nothing he takes is worth being injured or killed for." This advice from Detective Jack Meeks is standard for urban children. Many I talked with have learned it early.

"Nobody cares whether you get beat up or not, they just want your money," one boy told me.

"What do you do when they ask you for it?" I asked.

He mimics: " 'Hey, kid, you got any money?' We say no and walk away. They rarely follow us. When we say no, they use bad language and usually go away."

The thrust of police advice is to prevent children from getting themselves into a position that is likely to make them victims of a crime. No set of rules or guidelines offers complete safety. The goal for parents is to teach an informed approach which will help children avoid trouble and minimize the bad effects of whatever problems they may encounter.

"When an older kid or a bully comes up to a kid and says 'Gimme a quarter or I'll punch your face in,' the same logic applies as it would to an adult. Their safety is worth more than the money," says Detective Thomas Oates. "We tell kids the same thing we tell adults: 'You are more important than property.' We also tell them that any incident should be reported to parents or to the school.

"If a crime is under way, we tell people to follow whatever their natural instincts tell them to do," says Police Officer Terry McGill of Portland, Oregon. He adds, "There are too many variables to give pat advice on how to handle all situations."

"People are very different," Oates agrees. "You can't teach everyone to fight. They are going to follow their own inclinations. Some people have a natural ability to strike out and others do not. They will find other ways to deal with a situation. Everyone has to do their own thing when confronted."

"Judgment" is a difficult concept for children to grasp—and an even more difficult one to learn. Yet there *are* options how to behave in certain situations, and children need to learn what they are. Knowing that some, if not all, the choices they want exist, should make children better able to handle themselves with minimum risk.

It is important for children to have confidence in themselves, but they should never become so confident that they court avoidable danger and potential tragedy. Children should neither overestimate their physical prowess nor underestimate the capabilities of attackers. The first priority is always to be on the alert for a chance to escape.

It is hard to learn how to avoid confrontations and how to remain calm when you cannot avoid them. Sometimes it seems to children that risking danger is preferable to being embarrassed. One teenage boy told me that a few years earlier, as he was walking near a group of boys from out of his neighborhood, he overheard one of them say, "OK, that's the one. Get him."

"I would have felt like a fool if I had run. Either way, if I ran or stayed, they would win. One of them grabbed me and said, 'Gimme your money or I'll break your arm.' I gave him my money. Then they told me to run away. I started to run and then I got mad and I went back and started to run after them. Then they started to run."

He felt a little better after he chased them, even though this was not the safest action. When he described the incident, he realized it would have been better if he had run away in the first place. He probably would not have been mugged.

Children sometimes can feel that to confront a dangerous situation will be less of a catastrophe then to call attention to themselves. Because of the need to be "cool," they consider it more embarrassing to be thought of as stupid or different in any way. Young adolescents often have not yet learned to trust their judgment. Even though this boy knew it would have been better for him to run away and avoid the situation, he was reluctant to act on his knowledge and look like a coward.

It is hard to help children learn that such feelings are natural, but not necessarily smart from the point of view of their safety. Teens and preteens need to understand that having run away from danger will not make them social outcasts. But parents frequently realize that their older children do not believe that others, especially parents, understand situations the same way they do.

One way to avoid the appearance of lecturing is to talk about these matters in terms of your own experience and feelings. With older children, it is hard not to sound preachy if you try to issue too many "rules." Teenagers often seem not to listen or even to be hearing what you have to say. But they hear more than is at first apparent. If you have had earlier safety talks and established family policies when children were younger, your task will be easier because you will have something to build on. But it will never be easy. There are no simple rules to follow, and sensible improvisation is hard to teach. Fortunately, things change as children get older. "I'm glad I got big," said one boy who had been mugged frequently when he was younger. "No one has mugged me since I grew up. I try to be careful and not to walk alone at night. It's stupid not to go two blocks out of my way to a safer street, if I have to. I don't want to do anything stupid anymore.

### Things to Remember If You Are Confronted

1. Give up your property. Do not fight for it.
2. If a mugger has a knife to your throat or a gun to your head, talk to the mugger in a very soft, almost inaudible voice. You are trying to get him to relax and listen so he will only take your property and leave without hurting you.
3. A mugger is nervous and in a hurry.
4. Try to stay calm. Concentrate on getting a description of the mugger—height, weight, age, complexion, hair, any special characteristics.
5. Get away as soon after as possible.
6. Report it to the police immediately.

Both boys and girls should be aware that fear is a natural human trait from which nobody is exempt. During your talks with your children, admit there are times when you have been fearful. Point out that fear can be a signal that warns you of potential dangers, just as pain can be a signal that something is wrong in your body. Try to teach them never to be ashamed of acknowledging their fears to themselves. Fear has a place in safety discussions. No one likes to admit to being afraid, you can say, but fear has constructive uses. It has saved lives in the past and will continue to do so. You might point out a time, if you can think of one, when acting sensibly on legitimate fear has saved you from harm.

Tell children that acknowledging fears does not mean that they are fearful people or cowards, or that they should dwell on fears or even tell their friends about them. It simply means that they will give them their due place in making decisions about safety.

It is important not to feel ashamed or foolish about being fearful in dealing with the realities of the street. Being alert, even suspicious, may prevent you from walking blindly into a bad situation. If more people acted with a bit of common-sense suspicion, a good deal of street crime could be avoided. Some caution can be used to your benefit. Children should be prepared to follow their suspicions by avoiding any known high risk areas or situations. And if they cannot be avoided completely, at least children should be alerted to be on guard.

Crime prevention experts agree that it is important for youngsters to act as if they are on guard and alert to what is happening around them. Such an outward appearance can serve as a protective armor. It sends out the message "I'm no easy mark." The way that children stand or walk can say to the world they know how to handle themselves. The child who is daydreaming, who counts the cracks in the sidewalks, who is tired or upset, who seems to be wandering around aimlessly or is not paying attention to the surroundings is more vulnerable to attack than one who is alert and seems at home in the environment.

A child who needs help on the street, advises Jim Cartier of the Texas Juvenile Justice Center, should look for someone in uniform, even if that person is a delivery truck driver. A person in uniform, any uniform, is more readily identified with some kind of service or support function. He believes such people are more inclined, sometimes even trained, to help because they have a philosophy more geared toward public service than those not in uniform. He says that someone in a three-piece business suit will be more likely to think, "You little—, are you trying to rob me?" Some companies deliberately encourage their uniformed employees to be public spirited and helpful to children. The very fact that they are identified by their uniform tends to give them a greater sense of responsibility.

Among the places Jim Cartier recommended children head for at times of trouble is the local post office. Most people think only of the police station or the fire house, but the post office can be of help as well. Children can be taught to remember it as one of their safe havens.

You should, however, caution your children generally not to expect help from strangers. Although some people may come to their aid, it is important for them not to become overly dependent on such help. Passersby often show a lack of interest or a reluctance to get involved. A boy who was mugged in front of a friend's apartment saw two elderly people come into the lobby. "They watched the whole thing," he told me. "At first I thought they should have come to help us, but then I realized that they were afraid for themselves and there was probably nothing they could have done anyhow."

The best forms of self-defense are those with little or no risk to the child intended to be a victim. Physical self-defense always involves the risk that the response might miss its mark, offer no effective protection and even enrage the attacker. For that reason, it should be used only as a last resort. The attacker is usually nervous and easily agitated. Not provoking him may avoid his resorting to violence and give a better chance of escaping unharmed.

There are, however, ways for children to defend themselves that do not involve physical contact or any special training. "Some kids get so scared when confronted by a mugger that they freeze up," said a police officer. They just stand there because they have panicked. It is natural under stress for the emotions to take over. It is very hard to stay calm and alert. The police say that the safest course—getting away—should be a first consideration.

At the same time, running makes sense only if there is a good chance of getting away by outrunning the mugger. If children run, they should flee to where there are other people, heading for a store or a busy street, where they can mingle with the crowd.

Another form of self-defense is to yell for help. It can be a good defensive technique, provided a mugger does not have a weapon at a child's throat. Then, soft quiet talk is called for.

If your child is calling for help, the best thing to yell is "fire" not "help." A yell for help asks others to get involved. A yell about fire implies that others are already involved. With "fire" there is a good chance they will want to know more; the odds are that they will pay attention in the interest of their own safety. Also, yelling "fire" may confuse the assailant.

## What to Do If You Are Being Followed

1. Cross the street.
2. If a car is involved, change directions so it will have to make a U-turn to follow you.
3. Vary your pace, walk faster than you have been.
4. Run toward the nearest lighted or populated area.
5. If possible, a good tactic is to pretend to see a friend; wave or call out to the person.

When you advise shouting, screaming or yelling, be sure to tell your child that there had better be someone around to hear. There is not much point in screaming in an empty parking lot. And, says Detective Oates, remember that an attacker can put his hands around your throat and really hurt you.

A metal whistle, such as the ones used by the police, can have the same effect as a scream or a defensive yell, and whistles have prevented petty thefts and muggings. But only children who are old enough to realize that these metal whistles are not toys to be used for fun should carry them. Moreover, their use is not without risk. It is important to be able to get at the whistle quickly. Few children have key chains that can accommodate whistles. They will not do much good in an emergency at the bottom of a book bag.

Sometimes children are advised to kick an assailant. But Detective Oates, pointing out that kicking will most often enrage an attacker, says, "You'd have to land a perfect shot to make it work." In a confrontation, most children would not be up to doing that—nor would most adults. "Don't do anything that is going to hurt you," Oates adds. "If you are going to do something that is supposed to disable an attacker, you'd better do it right. And that's hard to learn."

For a child involved in a confrontation, talking can be a better form of self-defense. "There are ways you can talk yourself out of situations," says New York City Police Officer Charles Bonaventura. "It doesn't mean you are a sissy if you don't come home with a black eye. Talking has helped many kids through difficult times." He also tells about a young woman who said to a mugger, "How can you do this to me? I know your mother. We go to the same church." Her attacker went on his way because he thought maybe she did know his mother. But you have to use this kind of talk with care.

Many boys have reported using talking as an effective technique. One told me how he had coped with a mugging a block from his home. Four boys surrounded him, asked for money and started to "walk" him past his apartment building. They went right on walking, and "I just kept talking," he said. "It made me less nervous."

When one of his muggers lifted up his shirttails and showed a gun, he did not know whether or not it was real. "Have you ever seen one of these?" the boy asked him. He does not remember whether he said yes or no, but he managed to keep on talking. He recalls he was afraid he might laugh at some points and make them angry, adding that he frequently has the urge to laugh when he is nervous or in a tight spot. Talking helped him to fight panic. After a few more blocks, the boys got tired of "walking" him and, realizing that he had virtually no money, went away. He walked around the neighborhood for a while before he returned to his building, to make sure they had not come back.

Officer Terry McGill, former coordinator of the Youth Crime Prevention Programs of the Portland [Oregon] Police Bureau, agrees that talking can be a good tactic. He believes that, if a child can get a conversation going, the probability of physical harm will decrease. He advises parents that role-playing is a useful device—rehearsing with their children what they might say during a confrontation. Other parents may be more comfortable just talking about what a child might say and how to say it.

Lieutenant Nathaniel Topp of the Detroit Police Department suggests telling your child to try to move away while talking. "Don't just stand there, glued to the spot. If possible, back away." He suggests some responses a child might make: "I don't have any money, my parents have just been laid off" or "My parents are in the hospital. They had a bad accident" or "I was just on my way to ask our neighbors if I could do some odd jobs for them to earn some money."

When thinking about talking, there are some general points to bear in mind. First, if someone comes and asks for your money, answering with a flat "No" can sound confrontational or even hostile. If you add something, such as "But I wish I did" or say simply, "I'm sorry I don't have any" or "I don't even get an allowance," it sounds more conversational, which is the way you want to sound.

Second, it is crucial to avoid anything that defines what is really going on, such as saying, "Don't try and mug me, I have no money." Above all, you don't want to say anything that will make a mugger more nervous or make the situation more dangerous by inadvertently urging him to live up to your fearful expectations.

If someone asks the time, which can be a prelude to a mugging, you can try to ignore the question. This may work some of the time, but then you may hear, "Hey, man, I'm talking to you." If you don't feel you can run away, it is then usually wise to answer. Instead of a flat, I don't know," a child can say, "I don't have a watch" or "I had one that broke."

Talking will not always work. But knowing it as one strategy to try can be helpful.

There are two ways of talking that will definitely *not* work and might make things worse for your child, the experts caution. First, never talk tough or threateningly. A mugger may respond to it as a challenge. In the strain of a bad moment, a child might be tempted to pretend toughness and to talk big. Caution against this firmly and explicitly.

Second, it is not smart to plead or act weak, thus inviting contempt. It makes the mugger think he can get whatever he wants from an easy mark.

Crime prevention experts also suggest that it is generally better to ignore insults, personal and racial slurs and threats as well as verbal challenges or dares. They may make a child angry—quite appropriately—but it is far safer not to overreact and get sucked into a verbal altercation that is likely to turn physical.

If your child is walking alone and is taunted by other

youths, returning the insults will probably make him the loser to superior force and numbers. He may find it hard to walk on saying nothing, but in such situations caution is the better part of valor. In discussing this, you should point out that you sympathize with his legitimate anger and that there may be occasions when a response in kind is right and proper; but keeping cool in a potentially threatening situation may actually enable a potential victim to walk away untouched.

There are other tactics for children to try. Ed Muir says that if a child can carry it off, acting crazy under the threat of a mugging can be a good defense. In doing this a youngster might use non-sequitors, such as "Look out for fire engines," when there are none. The advantage of doing this is that the intended victim becomes an unknown quantity and even a potential threat. "Muggers do not like to deal with crazies," Mr. Muir says.

One woman I spoke to still remembers that when she was about 12, walking with two friends, they were confronted by three older boys who demanded money. She started to laugh hysterically; she could not stop. Fortunately, her two friends were smart enough to tell the muggers that she was just visiting them from a mental hospital. "Don't mind her," they said. "She is always like that." Confused and uncertain about what to do when a crazy girl was involved, the muggers went away and left them to go on their way.

But such a sophisticated approach can be tricky; it calls for a good deal of self-control, fast thinking and a bit of convincing acting skill. It is not for everyone.

Police officers report that some children have put their fingers into their throats to make themselves vomit, others have faked heart attacks or fits and some girls have pretended to faint. A technique that worked well for some ninth graders taken hostage by a crazed gunman in their Long Island school was to feign or induce nausea. They were among the first freed.

## When You Ride in a Subway

1. Always sit in one of the middle cars where there are usually more people and a conductor.
2. Do not sit in the first and last cars, unless you are traveling during rush yours.
3. Avoid empty cars.
4. Avoid long, dimly lit tunnels and entrances.
5. Do not stand near the edge of the platform.
6. Stand as close to the token booth as possible, especially if there are few people. Wait until you hear the train approaching to put your token in the turnstyle.

Crime prevention experts suggest that children be told not to carry all their money in one place. Keep it spread around. It you are confronted, you can express some hesitancy at first and then "Give them what you've got in your right front pocket or wallet," says Terry McGill. "They don't know where else you have it." Since most muggers are in a hurry, the risk involved in holding back is usually worth taking.

Several boys I spoke to have gained some personal satisfaction from not giving up everything, by having some additional money hidden away in shoes or socks. One youngster reported that he felt better because he never gave muggers everything he had. Another told me, "I got mugged for $3 when I had $7 with me. I felt like I got some of my own back."

To help your child stay calm during an incident, he or she should concentrate on memorizing the details of what actually happened. A child may not be able to prevent an episode, but may be able to help bring the mugger to justice and, as a result, feel better.

Police officers suggest that in recalling details, you proceed in an organized fashion, beginning with the head and working your way down. This head-to-toe action helps you to remember more when you are describing the event afterward.

Whether or not an offender is known to the victim, your child should try to note the time and place of the incident. Among the information essential to the police will be the attacker's sex, race, approximate age, height, build, hair type (color, thick, thin, etc.) and complexion. They will also want to know any particular words or phrases used by the mugger; a dialect or a tone of voice; any noticeable personal characteristics such as moles, scars, missing teeth, oddly shaped nose or fingers, or other blemishes. In order to make an arrest, the police need an accurate description of the offender. Understandably, in the excitement and panic of an ugly event, a child or an adult can find it hard to remember many details. The police also suggest that as an aid, you can compare a mugger to yourself. Is he taller, shorter, heavier, older?

An example of a helpful description might read something like this:

*Male, white, ruddy complexion, about 25 years old, between 5' 6" and 5' 8", 135 to 165 pounds, medium build, dark curly hair, sideburns, small moustache. Wearing a brown and white checked cap, no coat, blue shirt, dark pants and sneakers.*

Other useful details are the direction of the offender's flight, whether it involved a car and, if so, any information about it. If possible get the license number, color and make. The amount of remembered detail will, of course, depend on the child's age and emotional state. But impressing on children the importance of remembering as much as possible about a mugger increases their powers of observation during an incident.

After the event, write down as many details as possible while they are fresh in your child's mind even before these details can be told to the police. The very prospect that such testimony can help to punish a wrongdoer will encourage your child to improve his or her concentration.

As indicated earlier, it is very tempting to think that your children can be helped to fight street crime through formal lessons in self-defense. Much depends, of course, on the nature of such courses and the age and size of the child. But in general there are crucial points to watch out for. Stay away from any self-defense course that does not emphasize avoidance over actual fighting. "The first thing a child has to learn is when to resist and when not to," says Ken Glickman, a black belt at the World Seido Karate Organization in New York. Children can be too easily swayed by the macho and romantic attitudes of seemingly well-intentioned adults. Body-contact self-defense in the hands of amateurs, and particularly children, can be dangerous.

Most of the crime prevention specialists I spoke to are not opposed to the teaching of preventive self-defense tactics. They favor the lessons that teach children self-discipline. But there are limitations to any kind of physical self-defense for both children and adults, says Detective Oates. To be truly proficient, he adds, you have to make a lifetime study of karate and the other martial arts. He also issues a general warning. "I just can't believe these people who tell you to use keys in someone's face or to spray hair spray. It is extremely unlikely that you will do anything like disabling an attacker. You will probably just make him angry."

If this warning is kept in mind, there are some positive elements to learning self-defense. Classes can give a feeling of self-confidence and a better knowledge of how to handle the body. Such skills offer a real advantage as long as children understand their limitations in the face of deadly weapons or superior strength and numbers. Detective Jack Meeks reminds parents that children must know not to put up a fight against a knife or a gun.

Other experts caution that courses in self-defense, improperly taught, may give children a false sense of security. Both you and your children should keep in mind that a little knowledge, poorly used, can be more dangerous than none at all. One or two karate classes should not create the illusion that a youngster knows how to defend himself.

A sensible self-defense course, however, can give a valuable boost to a child's ego. Prevention strategies should be taught and explanations offered why certain tactics are right and others are not. And, of course, there is little point at all unless a child attends class regularly, practices the suggested techniques and pays attention.

I visited a few special self-defense classes for children and found that some of the older students (aged 11 or 12) were clearly benefiting from them, but I had serious doubts about their usefulness for younger children. Classes typically began with warm-up exercises, a workout and a review of earlier lessons. In one class, the instructor talked during the review. "Everyone knows why we use our knuckles? So you can't hurt yourself when you punch." He stressed the need for strengthening wrists and fingers and used the phrase "no pain, no gain." Different holds were practiced, sometimes with the instructor, sometimes between the children themselves. It was unclear whether most of the children understood the finer points of the holds and kicks.

"Basically, we are teaching kids the same things we teach to adults, with a different emphasis. And learning how to fall without hurting yourself is easier for kids," said one black belt instructor who teaches children self-defense at a local Y. "We also tell them not to practice on their brothers and sisters at home, only to work in class. Sometimes they don't listen when you say, 'Please don't throw that at my head.' "

# Protect Yourself*

Read the statements 1–15. Place the letter of the protective action you should take in the blank. Answers on p. 100.

*Protective Actions*

_____ 1. Someone is following you in a car.

a. Call parents, neighbors or police.

_____ 2. You see a friend hitchhike a ride.

b. You are vulnerable to crime.

_____ 3. A stranger telephones when you are home alone.

c. Move and tell an usher.

_____ 4. You ride your bike to the store.

d. You are the victim and should call the police.

_____ 5. You have birthday money.

e. Mark it for identification before you wear it.

_____ 6. You are baby-sitting and the child gets hurt.

f. Remember what you saw and report it to police.

_____ 7. You must take your house key to school.

g. Dial "O".

_____ 8. A stranger says that he or she has been sent to take you home from school.

h. Turn and run in opposite direction.

i. Copy down license number and call police.

j. Tell them your parents are busy and please call back.

_____ 9. A stranger bothers you in a movie.

k. Leave it at home in a safe place.

_____ 10. Your bike has been stolen.

l. Wear it inside clothing.

m. Call parent to make sure.

_____ 11. You have just witnessed a crime.

n. Lock it properly.

o. Try to talk your friend out of it. If you can't, do not go with him or her.

_____ 12. You are playing in an empty building.

_____ 13. You need to call for help, and there is no telephone book.

_____ 14. You have just gotten a new jacket.

_____ 15. Your friend wants to shoplift.

*Courtesy: Tips Program
Jefferson Bldg. 4th St., N.W.
Charlottesville, VA. 22901

Another class I observed was conducted by Tamar Hosansky and Pamela McDonell, co-directors of the Safety and Fitness Exchange (SAFE) in New York. They believe they "are giving kids a tool they can work with." They maintain that every child can benefit from learning some basic physical techniques and that even young children can improve their coordination and self-reliance by taking their courses. Their basic goal is teaching children how to handle themselves on the street, and instruction is designed to stress escape and survival techniques and play down combat. Classes at SAFE include time for children to talk about any frightening or difficult experiences they may have had during the previous week.

Other self-defense classes claim to improve mental concentration as well as physical responses, and in some cases, parents report that as children became more confident, their school performance improved as well. But most of the elementary school children I spoke to seemed unsure if the instruction was doing them any good. They were taking courses because "My mother wants me to" or "My father told me to." One 10-year-old said, "It seems like another sport to me."

One class I watched that featured creative safety games deteriorated several times into a free-for-all. Most of the children, seven and eight years old, seemed to agree between shouts with one boy who kept asking, "When are we going to play dodge ball?"

If you feel your home safety lessons need a boost from outside expertise, a general self-defense class which emphasizes prevention and common-sense avoidance can be useful. But you should be careful when training is in the specifics of the martial arts. Junior league self-defense has its pitfalls. An after-school recreation director, who has worked with children for more than 20 years, believes that the majority of elementary school children are not mature enough to understand these sophisicated concepts. This kind of training features a physical approach to problems. Most children still need to learn more civilized methods. Martial arts training is appropriate, he says, when children are about 12 years old. By then, they have developed the maturity to use the skills in a positive way. Ed Muir believes learning these techniques is good for teenagers, especially if they have already been victims.

Bear in mind also that many self-defense schools will not accept young children. And there is always the possibility that, if instructors are insensitive, a youngster could become unduly fearful or have nightmares from repeated warnings about attacks.

In other words, it is important to shop very selectively for a suitable self-defense class. If possible, visit some classes before you enroll your child. Ask the person in charge to explain the philosophy and see if you are comfortable with it. In general, the older the child, the greater the chance that he or she will benefit from the instruction.

Most of the children I spoke to said they liked their classes but, very sensibly, wondered if they would know how to use their new knowledge in a "real" situation. A teenage boy whose friend had taken karate reports it has given his friend renewed confidence in the wake of a bad experience. But he added that his friend "wasn't stupid enough to try to defend himself against a mugger who asked for money at knifepoint."

The question of whether or not to fight an attacker remains controversial, even when applied to adults. The decision is strictly a personal one, based on judgment about a particular situation and the capacity of the individual.

Police experts point to research showing that those who did not resist weathered criminal episodes unharmed more often then those who put up a fight. But the idea of physically defending your rights and standing up for yourself, no matter how dangerous the situation, is still appealing, regardless of the statistics. Often, it is the people who have not personally been victims in any kind of incident who strongly advocate a physical response to muggers. But my research and consideration of the problem have convinced me that the traditional avoidance-based methods of self-defense for children are sensible and safe. The odds are better with this conventional approach that a child will not be harmed, say the police department crime prevention units.

Admittedly, those who advocate fighting an assailant have a strong theoretical case. Neither we nor our children should have to restrict our activities or our lives in fear of becoming victims. But I find it difficult to deal with these matters in theoretical terms. In practice, I did not want my children alone in the playground when they were younger, nor did I want them to come home after dark.

For children of all ages, I accept the conventional wisdom of the police, whose job it is to protect us and who deal realistically with problems. I may not like all the advice they offer, and I certainly do not like the necessity for such caution, but I must agree that they are telling me how to deal with the real world. It is irresponsible and dangerous to disregard practical experience and to advise young children to try, David and Goliath style, to rout a larger and stronger adversary. This seems to be a risky way of setting them up for a painful failure.

It cannot be stressed too often to children that intuition, sixth sense or just plain "funny feelings" constitute a natural warning system, and they should always pay attention to such feelings. When children feel uneasy in a situation, there is probably a good reason, even if the reason for such vibes is not immediately obvious. And the fact that a child seems alert may even deter a potential mugger.

Tell your children that using their brain is their most important natural defense, more powerful than their fist. Such advice should be particularly welcome to the parents of boys and girls who are not "born athletes." Athletic prowess is no precondition for successful self-defense. In fact, except for being able to run quickly, it has very little to do with how well they can protect themselves.

Their minds and their intelligence will help children evaluate each situation and determine how they should act. Thinking about their true capacity will help them act calmly with self-confidence and self-control.

# ■ 6 ■

# Help the Child: The Victim Is Not to Blame

IT happened on his own street as he was coming home late one afternoon. Alex was 10 at the time. Two grown men held a switchblade knife to his throat and asked for his money. He had only a little small change. The worst thing, as far as Alex was concerned, was that they made him take off his belt and hand it over so they could see he was not hiding any money in it. It had been his first grown-up belt. When they saw that he had no more money to steal, they took his soccer ball and then let him go.

His mother reports that Alex was chased or mugged at least three other times between the ages of nine and twelve, usually when he was carrying packages. "He learned to run fast when he sensed trouble," she said. "He kicked and ducked and ran. He developed a crazy kick backward that seemed to work." He took karate for a while after his first traumatic incident. She said she thought at times "he had the illusion he could defend himself." How much he learned, she was not sure, but he did develop quick, quirky motions which helped him against muggers.

Quite naturally Alex was upset and enraged after the bad experiences, feeling both helpless and humiliated. By the time he was 11 he became in effect a political conservative, interested in law and order. He passed through his "pro-war years, which were very hard for us," his mother said. He became a hawk and a fanatic about rules—the kind of child who would not ride his bike even a few yards in the wrong direction on a one-way street. He no longer agreed with any of his parents' beliefs, which were politically liberal. He also started to collect models of weapons and for years afterwards kept swords and knives in his room.

Alex decided to study German in fifth grade so he could read about the Nazi side of World War II. His mother reports that they "still have expensive military histories of World War II at home." He would not listen to any of their liberal ideas. "We did not know till years later about the extent of his collection of replica weapons. After he turned 13, he began to outgrow this phase, but it was terrible when he was in middle school."

As he got older, Alex packed away his collections, but he did not give them away. When he went off to college and a friend of his parents stayed in his room, they found the weapon collection still under the bed.

Alex's parents had tried to help, but they made several classic mistakes. They did not encourage him to talk with them about his feelings (admittedly difficult for both sides) because they felt inadequate and unprepared. "We comforted him the best we could," his mother told me, "but what can you say? We told him they (the muggers) were poor and probably on drugs." (This rationalization of the muggers' behavior was not helpful at all.) The parents did call the police and gave a detailed description of the culprits, but the police were unable to locate them.

Such stories show that many well-intentioned efforts tend to fail rather than help children who have been mugged.

Since a mugging is, after all, a very unsettling and demeaning experience, it is not surprising that in its aftermath children continue to feel terrible for some time. The reason these incidents don't get reported as often as they should, says Oregon police officer Terry McGill, is that they are such an affront to a child's dignity. "And with children, bad incidents are harder to take. They feel the pain more strongly than adults, who already have scars. The young hurt more. They have less to fall back on."

Talking about their experiences, other boys report feeling "incredibly bad," "like a wimp," "emasculated," and many other negatives as a result of being mugged. "They got away with it," one boy said. "I kept thinking I could have stood up to them. I felt like they were stronger than me."

"I was very scared after," another boy said, "because there might be one of his friends around. And I was really shaken up. I couldn't concentrate anymore." (That condition lasted about a month.) "It really felt strange. For the first time in my life I was really scared. I'd never been really scared like that before."

The mother of a nine-year-old who was mugged at knifepoint told me that for a while the boy was more "excitable" than usual. He was hesitant about going out and willing to be driven to school for about two weeks. Then he was ready to resume walking. For a while, the mother said, laughing as she recalled it, he "dressed like a mugger" at home with a leather jacket and kerchief she did not like. But it passed. The bad experience, she said, did not teach him to "give in." In fact, he wanted to carry a pocketknife for self-defense, and she had to go to great lengths to explain that the boy who mugged him was prosecuted because he had a knife. Her son had also wanted to use a weapon against someone he thought was stealing wood from their country house, even if it was a bow and arrow.

Listening to children and their parents talk about muggings suggests a parallel with rape. In both crimes, the victims feel they have been trespassed on and violated while powerless to defend themselves. Mugging or any other form of robbery may not be as humiliating as rape, but it is nevertheless psychologically damaging, shocking and frightening. I was struck by the number of people who did not want to talk about past muggings, by the boys who, my sons report, never mention it, who are reluctant to go to the police, who feel humiliated or just want to put the experience out of their minds.

In both rapes and muggings, there seems to be the same kind of emotional response to being overpowered by someone bigger and stronger and shown your vulnerability by him. And interestingly, just as women who have been raped sometimes mistakenly assume part of the guilt, children often load themselves down with a big portion of the guilt for having been mugged. They tell themselves they were in the wrong place at the wrong time or, as one boy put it, "I shouldn't get caught in these situations. I'm someone who is not too smart. If I was smarter, these things wouldn't happen. Deep down I feel it is my fault."

Some incidents might perhaps have been prevented by "smarter" behavior and by adhering to all the safety rules given by parents and schools. But nothing should shift the guilt away from the real guilty party, the mugger. Children should not feel responsible for any part of the incident, and it is up to parents to make sure they do not. Kids suffer enough mental stress after having been mugged, without having to face any misplaced guilt.

It is vital that parents not inadvertently send out any guilt-producing messages, such as asking "Why were you there at that hour?" Teaching children to avoid certain situations as a means of preventing trouble is, as stressed earlier, quite a different matter from appearing to say after the event that the mugger had a right to be in a certain place and the child did not.

Children may remember a mugging as a disappointment to their parents, suggests New York psychiatrist Sirgay Sanger. "It is important for children not to see themselves as bad in this instance," he says. "They may not have followed all your safety instructions, but in so many cases they can get mugged even if they have been careful. The important thing is for them not to feel they have disappointed you or been failures because they were victimized in an incident."

A child may look at matters from a somewhat different point of view. One boy I spoke to who has been mugged and "bothered" about 10 times has given the matter some thought. "If you think of it as your fault, then you have some control over it. It is a way to survive, you give yourself control that way. It's a way to get by and not go crazy. Without an interpretation like that, it would be hard for me to go out at all."

"To blame yourself for being in the wrong place at the wrong time is quite common," says Steven Levenkron, a New York psychotherapist. "Self-blame makes the victim feel more powerful. That is why we see it happening frequently with rape victims as well as children who have been mugged.

"If women or children are attacked and then blame themselves for being on that dark street alone, what we are really seeing are people who don't want to think an attack could happen every time they walk out on the street. So what they have done is construct a situation where they tell themselves they have made so many errors that they deserve to be assaulted. Unfortunately, to blame yourself is not a realistic way to feel powerful. You don't protect yourself that way.

"You don't stop feeling bad either," he adds. "Parents need to help children stop feeling any inappropriate guilt and not to inadvertently add to it, by making any excuses for the mugger.''

By way of counseling, Levenkron says, you want to help the victim be angry at the person who did the mugging. "Children, like adults, often need to talk this through as a means of getting help with being angry at the perpetrator. That is the healthiest outcome. Then they can take appropriate action. Being forced to hide the anger spells trouble."

He cites the example of a patient who blamed herself when she was attacked, saying, "I shouldn't have been at that subway stop." She lost touch with her anger and became fearful and almost paranoid about going out. She saw everyone as a potential attacker and was afraid to leave whenever she came for treatment. After therapy made it possible to her to express her anger at her assailants—the real villains—she was able to face the streets again and to function normally.

One reason why it is sometimes difficult for children—and their parents—to feel appropriate anger is the tendency to sentimentalize the muggers, just as the mother cited earlier in this chapter romanticized muggers as poor people trying to get their share. It did not make her son feel any better.

"Deal with facts," advises New York pediatrician Edward A. Davies. "That other person is a bad apple. He is just plain aggressive and greedy, and will do whatever he has to do, including hurting others, to get what he wants. Muggers don't function within the framework of normal human behavior.

"The problem with mugging and stealing in general in our society is that many people think it is a right of the poor. In some societies, the poor do have the right to steal, but not to commit violence. In America we have sentimentalized crime, saying this is the way poor people have of getting even. We do not think enough about the victim's rights.

"It is a mistake to tell kids, 'What can you expect? This is a poor boy.' Does this give someone the right to say, 'Give me your bike or I'll beat the daylights out of you?' I don't think it does. We can sympathize with poor people in general, but I don't think we should sympathize with muggers."

Daily newspapers sometimes offer extreme cases of how people can be sentimental about crime and criminals, even where children are the victims. One example: A Long Island man, Robert Wickes, was despondent over his recent dismissal as a school aide; he shot the principal and a student at a junior high school, and then held a class of 13-year-olds hostage in the school for several hours. When it was all over, a neighbor commented about the criminal. "He lost the job and that embarrassed and humiliated him. School kids can be very cruel. Bobby's a kid himself; he was trying to do a job, and something happened that caused him to lose his self-respect and his belief in people. It must have crushed him when he lost that job."

Most people would not go to that extreme in excusing criminal behavior. But some parents are letting their political ideologies make them believe that deep down the mugger is merely a good guy who had gone wrong.

"There is more of a problem for children when we don't recognize the mugger as a bad guy," says Dr. Davies. "Kids have less trouble recovering if they know muggers are the bad guys. You don't have to be afraid of them, but you have to watch out for them and identify them. They are like tigers in the streets. You have to know about them.

"You can then say with true conviction to a child who has been mugged, 'That's really terrible. People should not do that to other people. The guy who did this to you was wrong. This shouldn't happen. We've got to do what we can to help stop it.' "

Both you and your child have a right to be angry. In addition, parents should point out to their children that the majority of poor people are not thieves or muggers, but law-abiding citizens. To teach children that poor people should be helped out of their poverty does not mean to excuse anti-social or criminal behavior.

Another fairly common, unfortunate misconception is the idea that experiencing severe fright is a potentially toughening experience. It is as absurd a notion applied to children as to adults. Dr. Lenore Terr, a psychiatrist who teaches at the University of California in San Francisco, has studied the aftermath of the Chowchilla incident when 26 California schoolchildren, ages five to fourteen, were kidnapped on their way to a swimming outing in July 1976. They spent more than a day in a state of terror and anxiety before their ordeal ended.

From her studies of the Chowchilla children after their traumatic experience, as reported in *The Washington Post,* Dr. Terr has concluded that a frightening experience of "extreme psychic trauma forces an individual to spend time and energy playing, dreaming, reenacting very mundane and trauma-related things. And it narrows his life philosophy."

For example, Dr. Terr found that the children in her control sample, when asked to describe their fears, mentioned things like earthquakes or nuclear war. But the Chowchilla children did not mention earthquakes, wars or accidents. Some reported how much more frightening the kidnapping had been than any earthquake could be.

"Severely traumatized children do not ignore issues of world concern because they are tough," Dr. Terr said. "Instead they narrow their spheres of concern to such items as their own rooms at night, to things closer to home." During the first year after the kidnapping, in addition to directly related fears, "there were more mundane fears, such as being outside alone, and fear of the dark. . . . It looked like they had lost their trust altogether, their sense that they could trust the world.''

This was an extreme situation, the kind of traumatic event that children do not ordinarily face. But many who have lived through their own less dramatic, frightening experiences have had some of the same reactions to a lesser degree and for a shorter time.

Thanks to Dr. Terr and other researchers, there is increased interest and knowledge about how children react to stressful events. We have learned to realize that they may as readily be subject to delayed stress as adults, even though not enough is known about children's acquired vulnerabilities, strengths and resiliencies. Frightening experiences will shake up all children in the beginning, but some will bounce back quickly; others will take longer. Some may become so seriously distressed they need special help.

In all cases we see great differences in how children react to stress in other situations as well. For instance, when children are hospitalized, some accept it well and others have trouble. Parents must keep in mind that children at risk, those who have faced bad situations, will benefit most from help and understanding. Never forget that when a child is a victim, it is up to you to make sure the experience will do no lasting harm.

What should you do if your child has been victimized?

Suppose a bike or some money is stolen. First and foremost, all the experts I consulted insisted, you help your child by starting a healing process as soon as possible. And just as important—do not let any of your own negative feelings of outrage or anger get in the way of concentrating on helping your child. Difficult though it may be to deal with your child after he or she has been mugged or molested, enter this situation as a parent. It was the child who had the bad experience. Keep your own emotions out of the child's way.

Parents are apt to make two common—and quite natural—mistakes after their children have been mugged. The first is to overreact and get hysterical on first hearing about the incident. If you say "Oh, my God, you could have been killed" or "You could have been maimed for life" or "You could have been raped" and go on with a list of terrible things that might have happened, you are making matters worse. You are teaching children to be frightened, which, of course, is quite the opposite of what you want to do. If you are fearful, you will communicate your anxiety to your children, whether or not you mean to. That is why it is so important to think through your own feelings and keep them under control.

"When a child has been victimized, no matter how, it is a damaging event in his life and he needs to be helped," says Terry McGill. "But parents should not overreact. Our responses can make kids feel it is a bigger deal for them than it is."

Another mistake many parents make is to go to the opposite extreme: withdraw and abdicate, telling themselves—and their children—"There is nothing I can do about this" or "I cannot deal with this." Such a defeatist attitude will make your child feel abandoned just at a time when you are needed most.

Some parents try to cope by denying their strong feelings of anger and irrational guilt for not having been able to protect their children. One father I spoke to after his son had been mugged told me that the boy had not actually been afraid. The father had talked to him quietly and the boy suffered no ill effects.

In another instance a mother dealt with her feelings of inadequacy by telling me, "I did not discuss the mugging with Richie. That's his father's area. He seemed to be OK." The child in the case was a 10-year-old boy who had been held up in New York's Central Park at knifepoint by a mugger who took his money, his watch and a book bag. The parents were unable to confront the possibility that their son might have been in real danger, so they denied that the event had been a traumatic experience for any of them.

I sympathize with parents not wanting to face the fact that their children could be in danger. I was out of town at a conference a few years ago when my younger son was involved in an incident. My husband dealt with the situation. I had to admit to myself that I was relieved at not having been there. Yet I rushed to speak to John on the phone, and after my return we talked about the experience. I understand the natural impulse of wanting to avoid talking about an unpleasant incident; I do not think parents should give in to what seems like the easy way out.

For a child it is most damaging *not* to talk about the incident, to be ashamed to report and discuss it, says psychologist Stephen Levenkron. Since children will often feel humiliated and inadequate after being mugged, parents must take a special effort to help them come to terms with their feelings. If children cannot talk about a bad experience with you, they will be robbed of an opportunity to work out their anxieties and feel better for it afterwards. Without this opportunity, they may discuss it only with friends, whose limited experience will not be very helpful, or not talk about it at all and bottle up the fear and anger.

Parents need to learn firsthand just what a bad experience has meant to the child. Dr. Sirgay Sanger suggests that you move cautiously, taking one step at a time. Begin in a conversational tone. Do not rush in with adult sympathy until you find out what aspects bothered the child most.

There are many ways for you to be reassuring. Affirm that it was not the child's fault. You can say things such as "You did everything you could" or "It would have been a big mistake for you to try and fight that guy. He was bigger and stronger than you" or "There were three of them and only one of you."

Terry McGill suggests such phrases as "I would have done the same thing in your shoes" or "If that happened to me, I would feel really low." This gives a child the feeling that you really understand and sympathize.

You may be tempted to say, "Why didn't you do such-and-such?" or "How did you let yourself get into a mess like that?" Such pointless after-the-fact criticism will be harmful to your child and to the relationship of trust you are trying to build.

Similarly, it is better not to say, "You should have been more careful" or any other such reminders. A youngster may have taken all the safety precautions you taught and still gotten mugged; or he or she may have forgotten some points. In either case, the child will feel worse. This is not the time to remind him or her to "be more careful in the future." In doing so, you invite the interpretation that you believe the victim was somehow responsible for what happened.

During the healing process, children need to reassure themselves that the incident will not happen again. After some time has passed without further trouble, the child will be gradually reassured and regain self-confidence. This will not happen overnight. It comes with a slow buildup of a sense of safety derived from the absence of any new unpleasantness.

Dr. Richard Rabkin, a professor of psychiatry at New York University, suggests that during your comforting talks—he calls them "debriefing" sessions—you let the child go over all the details of what happened at his or her own pace. Give the child as much time as needed to feel whatever he or she did was all right. The youngster will thus gain relief by getting the negative feelings into the open.

Often, Dr. Rabkin says, the most humiliating or troublesome details do not come out during the first account of the incident, particularly in the presence of other people who are not family members. A child should be made aware that the story can be told more than once—as often as necessary to get at all the facts.

You should be prepared for some tears and even a good cry, depending on the child's age and the severity of the incident. Let the tears flow and say whatever comforting words suit your own personal style. "It must have been really awful" or "That really stinks" or "What a s . . . thing to have happen."

Your child may, in the course of your talks, mention that there had been omens pointing to the mugging. One of the findings in the aftermath of the Chowchilla incident was the "discovery" by the children of "signs" which, they believed, had they interpreted them correctly, might have kept them off the fateful bus. One boy even believed the whole thing happened because he had stepped on "an unlucky square."

Another Chowchilla child remembered seeing a movie several years before with his father, who had asked him what he would do if someone pointed a gun at him. The child had not answered. After the kidnapping, he tortured himself with the idea that he had missed an opportunity to learn how to protect himself.

It is quite common for children to turn a troubling event over in their minds again and again, and to conjure up "omens" and fantasize about "if onlys." This is nothing to worry about; it should gradually lessen and fade away. Resist the temptation to say, "Don't be ridiculous" or "Omens are just superstitions," or otherwise belittle those thoughts. Children, and even adults, at times of stress can be forgiven for indulging in some supernatural thoughts. It is a way of trying to feel powerful in their imagination, when they are, in reality, powerless. Be sympathetic, but at the same time try to point out the realistic elements of the situation.

Also, try to help a child with a case of ''if onlys'' by being reassuring. Do not harp on the futility of that kind of thinking. It will not alleviate the distress. The child needs to be led to being angry at the mugger only, not at himself.

When your child is talking to you about an unsettling experience, remember that shame and humiliation are hard to discuss. It can also be hard for you to listen, but it will be worth your while. Your goal is to help make negative feelings easier to deal with by sharing them. Terry McGill tells parents not to play investigator and not to be mind-readers, but to respond to the child's feelings.

As a positive illustration, a mother told me her daughter had been attacked by some other girls. During the fight, her favorite jacket was badly torn. The mother suggested that they sew the rip.

''I never want to see that jacket again!'' her daughter told her, thus making this mother realize that she had been thinking only about the practical, superficial aspects of the situation—a jacket that had been quite expensive. For the daughter, the jacket was an integral part of an incident she wanted to put out of sight and out of mind.

After an unpleasant experience, during which they have lost a valued object or have been physically or psychologically abused, children may feel they are cowards or ''wimps'' or helpless victims in a harsh world. The episode can be relived many times. If left to fester, it can damage a child's self-image.

Once you have helped children express their feelings, they can then slowly stop agonizing over what they ''should have done'' or wanted to do and could not. You can help a child to evaluate the situation and put it in proper perspective, recognizing that to belittle such an experience as a "small" incident (even if it is) can be as harmful to a child as to overreact.

"I grew up in what was called a tough neighborhood and I know how it feels to be held up by bigger kids. It is a heavy trip and not something you forget easily," a friend told me. "Kids need all the support they can get." Wise parents will offer it.

## When Should You Seek Outside Help?

If after more than a month goes by and your child is still experiencing any of the following, you may want to consult a professional:

1. Disturbance in sleep patterns with recurring nightmares
2. Change in eating habits, particularly loss of appetite
3. Increase of physical complaints
4. Difficulties in school, either academic or behavioral
5. Reluctance to go out of doors
6. Marked changes in behavior that persist. For example, if an outgoing child becomes withdrawn or a well-behaved child begins to misbehave frequently.

The next question is a practical one: Do you buy your child another bike or radio to replace the stolen one? Yes, agree the experts I consulted. You wanted him to have it in the first place. Now, you want to protect him from unnecessary hardship in the aftermath. If you don't replace the bike, a child feels twice victimized. If you say, "Well, those are the breaks in life," you imply that having been mugged was the child's fault. You are punishing him on top of the punishment he has already suffered. It would be different if he had carelessly left his bike out overnight without locking it and you wanted to teach him a legitimate lesson.

Parents should be patient and wait for a child to get over the effects of a bad experience. This may take some time. Children may remain upset for several weeks, without cause for concern. It took one boy a month before he was able to settle down again and concentrate normally on his school-work. In general parents should handle such situations without rushing off to get professional counseling.

Only if after some time has passed a child develops phobias or does not want to go out or keeps having nightmares, or if faith in a just world is not being gradually restored—then the need for professional help may be indicated. But ordinarily, the best way to let the wound heal is for parents to offer comfort by answering questions, listening and giving reassurance until the child's natural optimism returns.

Another way to help children recover is to ask them what they would like to do about the bad experience. You can suggest constructive outlets for their anger. You may want to consider investigating some kind of self-defense course, if your child is old enough and there is a good one in your area. (See Chapter 5.)

If it seems appropriate, you can encourage your child to report the incident to the police or school authorities. This was an action that helped our son a great deal. Even if the thief is not caught, the child feels that he or she is taking a positive step toward stopping future threats and harassment. Trying to enforce the law is an antidote to feeling abused and powerless.

"We let kids who have been vicitmized come to the nearby San Jose station and talk to a police artist while he sketches," reports Police Officer Lori Kratzer of Palo Alto, California. "The children here are treated like adults, not like helpless victims." She believes that such treatment is part of their education. They become involved in the process of identifying their attacker and are better able to think rationally about the stress they have endured.

The decision about whether to call in the police should be based on your own personal assessment of the situation. It can be an important healing step, particularly if there has been a weapon involved and the crime is serious. As long as the mugger is still at large, he is free to prey on other children. While there is no assurance that the culprit will be caught, not reporting the incident simply means throwing in the towel—not a good civic lesson. When you take your case to the authorities, your child sees you are an active person, using the police department's resources to catch the bad guys.

As one boy put it, the mugger "could have kept going forever if he didn't get caught." Before the culprit was apprehended, this boy was quite naturally afraid that there would be more trouble. "I was glad he was finally off the streets and that he couldn't get me anymore." Given the current high crime rate, you cannot realistically tell a child that there will not be another incident. But you can do everything in your power to help prevent it.

Many police precincts have officers who specialize in dealing with children, and even ordinary police officers usually try to be sympathetic. Many families report that they and their youngsters were treated with a respect by the police. A positive impression can be a lasting one in a child's mind. A woman I spoke to, now in her early thirties, still remembers how well the police treated her when she reported a lost bike years earlier as a junior high school student.

Yet many parents are hesitant to report a crime, largely because they are afraid of possible retaliation by the mugger or his friends. In general, police representatives I have talked to insist that there is little cause to be afraid to register complaints. Not doing so perpetuates the aggression and intimidation. Identification is the first step in catching a criminal. Going to the authorities and making a report acts as a deterrent. "Some threats are real, others are idle talk, but for the kinds of crime we're talking about with kids, there is almost never a threat of retaliation," says New York Police Officer Charles T. Bonaventura.

"We don't see any retribution here in Oregon," Terry McGill reports. But he admits in other places it may occur. "Here, it especially does not happen if the juvenile court or the police get involved," he adds. "If we know they've threatened, we put the fear of God into them. We tell the young offenders, 'Don't be going back because we know who you are.' We are threatening them with greater harm than they could do others." But he believes it really depends on the groups you are talking about. "The rules are different for different groups in different places."

"You do assume a certain risk when you go after muggers and bullies," says Carole Garrison, an assistant professor of criminal justice at the University of Akron and a former policewoman. "You have to be willing to spare some time to confront the situation directly and agree to identify and be identified. In some communities, this is safer than others. Parents can well ask, 'Once I get involved will the police protect my child from future harassment?' I think this is a risk, but it is well worth taking." But many wonder "What if the mugger is let off" as so many are in the juvenile courts—"Will my child get beaten up or will my home be vandalized?" There are no easy answers to these questions.

Carole Garrison urges parents to consider whether the incident is serious enough to be taken to the authorities. Situations differ. In some cases you may want to report to the school instead. Or simply to comfort your child and let the incident drop.

Another problem about going to the police is that petty and minor crimes have what Dr. Garrison calls minimal resolution, which means that few culprits are actually detained

and little stolen property is retrieved. In smaller and more
affluent communities, there are more resources and more
time to pursue them. But even there, the record is not prom-
ising.

This is why Dr. Garrison believes there are times when
the police may seem indifferent, abrupt, or not as helpful or
understanding as they should be. This can result from a
heavy workload or the problems of an individual officer.
Basically, the police sometimes have to say to parents, "We
can't do anything about these small crimes. There is the reality that they are not high priority. In many instances, it is
not cost-effective for us to pursue minor crimes. There are
limits to what we can do to help." And she adds that there is
often police frustration, which can be perceived as indiffer-
ence.

If you do call the police and tell the responding officer
about an incident, it does not automatically lead to any action other than the filling out of a crime-complaint form.
What you are doing is letting the police know an incident
has occurred so that they will start to investigate.

The response of the police to a particular situation will depend on a number of factors. The officer must determine
whether a crime has been committed and, if it has, under
what legal category it should be classified. The age of the
offender is also important in determining whether certain
laws will apply.

In order to go further than the filling out of a crime-
complaint form, the victim and his or her family must indicate a willingness to press charges.

What happens when you call the police after your child
has a bike stolen? Officer Charles Bonaventura tells what to
expect. Police officers would come to your house or apartment or you could bring your child to the police station.
Sometimes you can make your complaint over the phone.

The incident would receive its proper crime classification, depending on the value of the item stolen and whether or not a weapon was involved.

The officers would question the person who made the call (the parent) about the episode. They would also question the child in the parent's presence, asking for an account of what happened in a simple, straightforward way, e.g., "I was riding my bike on—, These two big guys came up to me—." The child would be asked if he or she knew the attacker and to describe him in as much detail as possible. The description of the mugger and the bike are particularly important because the police need information to be able to identify the culprit. If the person cannot be identified, the case cannot be pursued. And the reporting is important because, as Charles Bonaventura says, "One description may be what enables the police department to put the puzzle together and catch the thief.

"Basically, the department operates on documentation. If we can put together a pattern in a particular area, which is what usually happens when people call up, our chances of success improve. We get a description of what happened, what the person looked like and, of course, a description of the bike. The information on the complaint report then gets turned in and goes to the crime analysis office to review.

"We now have the description. Two hours later, if things are ideal, the police sight your bike and the person on it." (Of course, things are seldom ideal. They may never catch the thief. Or the call may have come in too long after the event, which would interfere with success.)

"But in the best case," Officer Bonaventura says, "we will then give you a call. 'We have your bike. Did you give this person we found on it permission to ride it?' If you say no, he is locked up for possession of stolen property.

"If you press charges, we get your written corroboration statement, saying that you did not grant the individual possession of the bike. When all the identifications are proved, he can them be charged. We would be arresting him on the child's say so. What we basically need is enough information for the case to stick. We don't want it to be thrown out of court for lack of evidence.

"The child may have to testify in court. It depends on the seriousness of the case, whether or not there was a weapon involved. If so, it would be a more serious crime. It would also depend on the district attorney. If he has a strong-enough case to proceed without having the child in court, he will not call the child. If not, he may have to call the child."

Many parents, having read unfavorable reports about plea-bargaining, have doubts about the effectiveness of the criminal justice system, especially with regard to youthful offenders. But Carole Garrison explains that plea-bargaining may actually help in the prosecution of cases of special interest to parents. In serious cases, such as those involving rape, she says, a district attorney may want to spare a child the additional trauma of testifying. And in other cases plea-bargaining does not necessarily mean a lesser sentence. It could also mean a more easily obtained conviction, with a better chance that a young criminal will be locked up.

If you decide to press charges, as a practical matter you will have to be prepared to invest a good bit of time. Delays, postponements and repetitions of the same testimony and facts require sacrifices of everyone, including the police and the district attorney as well as the child who is a witness and his parents. The case should be serious enough to make it worth the effort.

"You also have to remember," says Ed Muir, head of school safety for the United Federation of Teachers, "We have a group of young criminals who are able to function because they figure they have the odds on their side. If you go to court, nothing is going to happen to them if they are underage.

"The juvenile justice system does not work unless you are dealing with a felony, rape, armed robbery or another serious crime. If your kid gets punched out with a bloody nose and ripped off with a shearling coat, the chances of anything happening to the offender are small. For a more serious crime, it is up to the people involved."

One father, who described himself as a "reasonably militant parent" with a "Yankee mind," decided to prosecute the boy who had held up his son and some classmates at knifepoint. "I feel in a serious crime—which this was because a weapon was involved—it is a citizen's normal function to persist," he says.

Many parents would not have pursued the situation because there had been no injury to the boys involved. This father told me that he was commended by the judge for his perseverance. This was one case where the mugger was stopped from terrorizing others and went to a state camp.

But even he said he understood why many others do not act as he did. "With all the adjournments and the harassments of delay, it is natural for families to get tired of being involved and want to drop the whole thing. The defense lawyers for young offenders in cases like this play to these feelings and find as many reasons for delays as possible, hoping the victim and his parents will be worn down and give up."

Parents considering going to court should not minimize what is involved in addition to time. "We went through several hearings, plea-bargaining and a tough judge. There is emotional wear and tear. When my son told the story of what had happened under oath, he admitted to the judge that he was scared." He had been taught, like every other city child, not to fight with someone who held a weapon. He followed what he had been taught to do and it worked out all right. The defense asked him why he did not fight and he replied that he had been taught not to.

The father commented that his son, like many other boys,

had not liked this advice, but he followed it when confronted by a threatening situation and found out it was the best course of action. His judgment was ultimately considered sound; the judge had agreed with his decision not to fight.

The trial showed both father and son in a strong light. The boy had gained positive reenforcement by taking part in the proceedings. As the parent of a minor, the father was able to stay in the courtroom during the son's testimony. Earlier when the boy went to identify the mugger in a police line-up and his father could not be present, his grandfather accompanied him instead. "It is wise for an adult to support a child in this kind of situation to the greatest extent possible," the father said.

One boy, who was nine at the time I spoke to him after he had testified in court, described his experience. First he went to speak to the assistant district attorney, who wanted to make sure that all the details of the case were clearly understood. The boy had to tell the same story he told the police and then "in court I told the judge the same things. My book bag, which had been taken, was evidence because it had my name on it. Someone had tried to rub out the name."

The judge asked him questions—what happened and how he had responded. "Sometimes we went over things twice. They asked me once if I thought the mugger was in the courtroom and I pointed him out."

The youngster was in court from about 8:00 A.M. until 2:00 P.M. with time out for lunch. Because his father also had to testify, he could not remain in the courtroom, and the boy admitted that he felt nervous as he testified for more than an hour.

When I commented on how hard this must have been for him, he explained to me patiently that he had told his story earlier to the police and lawyers as well as to his friends. He knew what he was going to say, so the experience was not as difficult as I had imagined. In fact, his mother told me he had wanted to testify. "I think if I hadn't testified," he said, "I'd have been shaken up for longer."

I said afterward that having an experience like that makes you grow up a lot. He answered, "You bet." It was unclear whether he was referring to the testifying in court or to the mugging incident itself.

Parents naturally wonder what they would do if their child were involved in a disturbing incident. It should be comforting for them to realize that not all the outcomes need be negative. Some of the lessons learned may overshadow the initial incident. Children's self-confidence and their ability to cope under pressure will be tested. Youngsters often respond with greater common sense than they or anyone else had thought possible.

When you take time to comfort and support a child who has been ripped off, frightened or hurt, you are making that youngster feel how important he or she is to you. If you take time away from your job to go to the police or to court, the message is loud and clear that your children come first—before your job or profession. You are demonstrating that you care. Sharing and weathering a child's bad experience can bring you closer together.

# ■ 7 ■

# Frank Talk About Sexual Abuse

CHILD molestation worries parents more than any other crime. There is no more hideous offense than the sexual abuse of a child. Even hardened criminals view child molesters with disgust and scorn. Although precise statistics do not exist, it is clear from reported cases that sexual abuse is more prevalent than most people realize, and it may be increasing.

"Close to two-thirds of all children who are victimized may not tell their parents or anyone else about it," says Dr. David Finkelhor, who recently directed a comprehensive study of the problem, focusing on 521 families in the Boston area. Some children, he says, fear being blamed by their parents, being punished by the molester or simply not being believed.

The study, financed by the National Center for the Prevention and Control of Rape, a branch of the National Institute of Mental Health, found that nine percent of the parents had children who had been sexually abused. But Dr. Finkelhor estimates that the total number of child victims might be as high as double the number reported. Some of the parents in the study had been sexually abused themselves as children: 15 percent of the women and 6 percent of the men. Of this group, one-third were victimized before the age of nine. Cases in the Boston study and elsewhere include only those that are reported and recorded. There is an unknown number of uncounted incidents of cases seen by private physicians which do not become part of any public record.

Many parents have misconceptions about this difficult subject. They think child molestation almost always means rape. But the issue is actually much broader; it covers any approach made to a child initiated for the sexual gratification of an adult. This definition includes emotional as well as physical assaults on children which fall short of rape, such as seduction, exhibitionism or unwanted intimate touching. Or children may be forced to look at an older person's genitals or asked to undress or expose themselves in some way. These episodes can be very emotionally damaging to a child, sometimes even as much as rape itself. In many incidents of sexual abuse, even though a child's life, physical health, virginity or innocence may not be at stake, his or her dignity and self-esteem may be severely harmed.

| What Parents Fear | What Is More Likely |
| --- | --- |
| A weird, dangerous stranger | Offense by a person they know (often a relative or a friend of the family). |
| One isolated incident | Frequent incidents taking many different forms. |
| Out of the blue | A situation that develops gradually over a period of time. |

| A violent attack | Subtle rather than ex-<br>treme force. Bribery<br>and threats rather<br>than physical force. |

Adapted from *No More Secrets: Protecting Your Child from Sexual Assault* ©
1981 by Caren Adams and Jennifer Fay. Reproduced by permission of Impact
Publishers, Inc. San Luis Obispo, California.

The Boston study also reaffirmed that a majority of parents wrongly believe sexual molestation is committed primarily by strangers. Previous studies have estimated that between 60 and 75 percent of child sexual abuse is committed by relatives, neighbors or someone else known to the child. Strangers were the molesters of children in only 33 percent of the cases among the parents who had been abused themselves as children; 67 percent of the child abusers had been relatives and acquaintances of their families.

In addition, the study pointed out that most parents cannot bring themselves to warn their children appropriately about the potential hazards of child molestation. This was true even though nearly half of all the parents studied—47 percent—knew of a child of either a family member, acquaintance or neighbor who had been a victim.

"Parents seem to be telling their children too little too late," Dr. Finkelhor says. "Kids need to know they can tell parents and other adults about it. They can only do this if it is first brought up by parents. Kids may not have the vocabulary for discussing it."

Only 29 percent of the parents in the study said they had talked explicitly about sexual molestation with their children. Apparently a great many parents do not discuss the issue because they do not see their own children as being in any danger, even though they acknowledge that this problem is widespread.

Many parents and many professionals point out that sexual abuse is a hard topic to raise because they believe it can easily and unnecessarily frighten a child. Yet a common pattern among parents in the study was to talk to their children about kidnapping and to think that they were simultaneously issuing a warning against sexual molestation without explicitly saying so. Parents would caution children about getting into cars or accompanying strangers to secluded spots. The idea of sexual abuse would be on their minds, but they would not specifically mention it.

The irony is that kidnapping probably frightens children far more than sexual molestation. The idea that someone might try to take them away from their family and not let them see mother, father or friends again seems far more terrifying than to let children know there are people who may try to touch their sex organs. Especially to a young child, with a rather vague knowledge of sex but a distinct picture of separation, kidnapping would seem a far greater threat.

Moreover, kidnapping is not as prevalent as sexual abuse, even though parents are more likely to warn their children about it. And many of those abducted are children taken by their own parents in the course of custody disputes.

Another reason parents in the study did not warn their children was that they considered them too young to be told about anything related to sex. When asked what they thought was the appropriate age, most parents in the survey answered nine. Unfortunately, children younger than nine can become victims of sexual abuse. Many parents knew this, but they rationalized the truth by saying their children were too young and could thus evade their discomfort when thinking about the subject. Once parents began postponing their talks to wait for the ''right'' age and time, many just kept on postponing.

''Since many parents discussed kidnapping with their children,'' Dr. Finkelhor said, ''it's obvious that they're not afraid to bring up potentially frightening subjects. Bux sex is embarrassing, and parents may feel that once they bring up the subject of abuse, they need to talk about many complex values involving sex.''

He is convinced, however, that it is quite possible for parents to discuss abuse without having to be overly concerned with sexual information. For example, he says, ''You can discuss the 'body zones' concept; that certain parts of children's bodies are off limits to other people, and that there are types of touches that make you feel good compared with others that make you feel bad. Parents can tell children that they have the right to say no to Uncle Joe if he touches them in this way. Kids often instinctively sense something in abusers' furtiveness that they might describe as 'yucky.' ''

Dr. Finkelhor urges parents to tell children not to let an older person put their hands in their pants or play with their private parts. Parents can also tell children that their bodies are their own, and they have a right not to be touched in ways that make them feel uncomfortable.

Obviously, much of the reluctance parents feel in discussing sexual abuse stems from their more general discomfort in talking about sex itself. Many parents find it very difficult to mention sexual topics of any kind to children. They often feel they lack the knowledge and vocabulary to speak comfortably about sexual matters. They are embarrassed and afraid of appearing ignorant or tongue-tied.

Unfortunately, some parents probably will never have open discussions about sex with their children. But in spite of that, they should not shirk their responsibility to give adequate warnings about sexual abuse.

Even for those parents who can talk about sex with their children, there is probably nothing tougher to discuss than the possibility of sexual molestation. How do you bring the matter up to a young child without alarming him or her? Can you pick up a cue when a six-year-old says Uncle Harry tickles her in a funny way? It is relatively easy to warn your child about the disreputable-looking stranger in the playground; it is quite another thing to talk about a relative or an acquaintance. But you can begin very simply along with your regular talks about safety. Sexual abuse should be part of all safety talks. You can say something such as "Somebody might do something that does not seem right. They may want to touch you when you don't want them to. Tell me about it."

Parents naturally hope their children will never have the experience of being molested; but hoping is not enough. Although parents cannot wholly control the environment in which their children live, there are steps to take which can help protect a daughter or a son (boys, too, are often targets).

The first step is the recognition that anyone could be a molester. Children, because of their lack of experience and their innocence, can fall prey to unscrupulous tactics. This is very different from being mugged. And in spite of the stereotyped image of the "dirty old man," molesters come in every size and shape, race and creed. It can be anyone—a stranger or a family member, an acquaintance, a babysitter, even a schoolmate. (Statistics to date have shown that the overwhelming majority of molesters are men.)

"Part of any prevention of child sexual abuse is to enable a child to feel that he or she can appeal for help from parents," says Dr. Finkelhor. When parents tell children about child sexual abuse, it opens this line of communication. "The mere fact that children feel confident they can go to their parents for help or information may make them less vulnerable to abuse."

"Parents are much more comfortable telling their children how to cope with someone who wants to take their money than telling children how to cope with someone who wants them to take their pants down," says New York psychologist Steve Levenkron. The vocabulary to tell a child how to decline being molested is important because children often may not know what they are supposed to do when someone approaches them. "First a parent has to be comfortable talking about what kind of behavior the molester will request from them and then explain what the child should do. And that's a very, very tough assignment."

But like most experts, Levenkron believes it is important for parents to make the efforts. "The long-term damage that is done when a child is molested results from his or her inability to share it with anybody, the inability of the child to express anxiety or shame and to develop a perspective on it.

"It scares the parents more than the child to talk about sexual molestation. It is harder for a parent to say, I believe, than for a child to hear. The parents confront the reality that this may happen to their child, which stops them from talking about it. They often identify with their child, using their adult knowledge, which makes them fearful for the child. As a result, there is no communication."

## The Risks of Ignorance

Work with children who have been molested suggests that the abuse could have been prevented in many cases if they had had prior instruction. Lack of knowledge and uncertainty about what to do can play a role in a child's victimization. Afterward, children often say:

- They were confused and misled by the offender's insistence that the sexual activity was proper and normal.
- They did not know they had a right to refuse.
- They did not believe they would be defended by other adults (including parents) if they refused or complained.
- They were thrown off their guard when the adult be-

haved in a way that they had never been led to expect.*

*Finkelhor, 1982

In any discussion of the matter, it is important not to make children feel that they are likely to be singled out as targets, but rather that you are alerting them to the kinds of sensible precautions taken by all careful people. As with your talks about mugging, it is best not to lay down a rigid set of "don't" rules, but to discuss protective measures over time, which to some degree are observed by all members of the family—parents and teenagers as well as children. Safety matters are best presented as important areas of family concern. A news item about an actual incident can be used as a springboard for realistic discussions.

Parents must be careful not to carry their warnings to excess. Children should never believe that all grown men are suspect. Tell them that people who interfere with the bodies or liberties of others are exceptions. Say that those few people who do not respect other people's privacy, who try to force their attentions upon others and who sometimes are attracted to children instead of to adults are "strange" or "weird"; they are sick and need help, but until they get it, they are a danger to others.

Point out that people who care about their bodies show them only to those they know and love. This is part of a child's learning that sexual activity is right and appropriate under certain circumstances, but not under others.

The level of communication you have already established with a child will influence the way you can talk about delicate matters. If you say merely, "Don't get into a stranger's car," you sound scary or domineering even though you don't mean to. Begin slowly with suggestions such as "If someone touches you in a way that makes you uncomfortable, you can tell them to stop it." Tell children it is all right to lift someone's hand off their bodies or that if people pretend to touch them by accident, it's OK to object. The idea is to begin with simple, straightforward advice so that you prevent new fears from entering a child's mind, and try to lessen any fears already lodged there.

You can take any drama and emotion out of what you are saying and minimize your own feelings of discomfort in several ways. First, some parents find it helpful to practice in front of a mirror or with a spouse or friend who also wants to talk to a child about molestation. In this way, you can help each other to overcome initial reluctance and find the right words and examples.

Next, try to be matter-of-fact, using such phrases as "These are things which can happen sometimes" or "There is something that concerns me and I'd like to tell you about it." Of course, you should always ask if there are any questions. There may be some, if not the first time you discuss things, then after some additional thought. You might try asking about questions a day or so later. If you are doing a rehearsal session with a spouse or friend, try to anticipate questions you are likely to be asked and think over how you will answer them.

Your goal is to make the child feel comfortable about talking to you as the person who can be trusted to set things right. If there are two parents at home, try to be honest and direct about which one is the most comfortable doing the talking on this subject. If both are equally comfortable— or uncomfortable—try to decide between you beforehand which one is going to do most of the explaining. Hesitation about starting often springs more from the parent's discomfort than from a child's lack of readiness.

One way to begin is to set the stage by talking about children who may be "bothered" by an adult or an older child. The specifics can come later. When you bring things up in a general way, you may find your child will respond with some particulars. If your child knows about the sexual parts of his or her body and knows that only parents, a doctor or a nurse can touch them, you may find no need to mention specific sexual offenses to a small child.

## Some Examples of What Might Happen to Children and How They Should Respond*

1. If someone wants a hug and you don't want to do it, you can say, "No, thank you."
2. If someone pats you on the bottom, you can tell the person, "Don't do that."
3. If someone wants you to sit on his lap, you can say, "Not right now."
4. If someone older wants to touch your penis, you can run away from him.
5. If a relative always wants to give a sloppy kiss, you can shake hands instead.
6. If someone grabs you through your clothes, you can say, "Stop, that's not OK."

*Adams and Fay, *No More Secrets.*

The older your children, the more likely they are to understand the meaning of sexual abuse. They have probably already heard scary stories about strangers. It is far less frightening for children to know what is likely to happen, for example, having their private parts handled or seeing someone else expose his genitals, than to leave things to their imagination.

Molesters often tell their young victims that the incident must remain "secret." Since the offender is likely to be an adult or at least an older person and because the offense usually is physically painless, the intimidated child tends to submit to the molester's demands. Unless a child already has instructions from you that such incidents must never be kept secret and that you should be informed immediately, he or she may not resist and will be unlikely to report the incident to you.

Most experts agree that instilling in a child a healthy sense of self is the most important protection a parent can provide against sexual molestation. Teach children about proper personal conduct and respect for their bodies. Give the body dignity by naming its parts to the child without embarrassment. After all, we teach children safety rules by saying, "Stay away from hot stoves" or "Don't touch the electric outlet." Is there any reason for not teaching them how to safeguard the sexual parts of the body as well?

Make it a family policy in this area that the words for the sexual organs are used in your home without being coy or evasive. Your own "special" names are an acceptable second best. Problems arise when parents can only speak of "down there" or use some other equally vague and misleading terms. It can be upsetting for children to think that there is no name for some parts of their bodies or that there is some dark secret about them that cannot be given a name or be discussed.

Often parents give children the proper labels for knees, toes and elbows and other parts of the body, but withhold or avoid those for the breast, genital or anal areas. The lack of names tells children it is not all right to talk about those areas, that you as a parent are uncomfortable naming them. Without unashamed designations, it becomes difficult to talk about the abuse of such organs in a way that will be sufficiently specific to be meaningful and rational.

"Some kind of language has to be developed that everyone is comfortable with. That takes all the emotional loading out of it," Steven Levenkron says. "Then parents can tell children 'This is what molestation is. This is how you can prevent it. But if it should happen, this is how you can tell me about it.' Developing a mutual vocabulary is a beginning task for talking about sexual abuse. What you are doing is creating a structure and a language where none existed before.

"If the child is a boy, 'penis' has to be a legitimate word in the household and if it's a girl, 'vagina' has got to be a legitimate word and be referred to appropriately for different reasons. Then parents have a base to build on.

"Later, when a parent wants to caution a child, it is easier to begin with the business of what a child does if someone picks up a dress or takes down pants. You can then tell them, 'If somebody touches your penis or your vagina, you can run away and come home and complain to us.' If you are very shy with a child, you can say, 'If someone touches you in an area where your bathing suit would cover, you should tell us.'

"Under your bathing suit or your underpants is still a little mysterious. If parents are comfortable with that, it is all right. But it is more effective to be more explicit. Your child will have more of a sense of safety and familiarity if you can name body parts straight out."

Levenkron illustrates: "Let's say a child comes home and says, 'Mommy, somebody touched me under my underpants.' You want to know more about what happened. Your child might need to tell you. As a parent, you are very upset. You want to know if your child has been injured or not. How do you really find out if there are no words for penis or vagina?

"You then ask, 'What did the person do?' The child only shrugs his or her shoulders. Children cannot be clear if the parent has never allowed the proper focus on the sensitive area involved. At that point, the child is understandably reluctant to say any more. He or she cannot explain because no provision has been made for any language to describe what has happened or what seems wrong and upsetting.

"To use clothing as a descriptive way to indicate an area

of the body is better than nothing, but it's a lot better to have the right names. I really believe that children should know their body parts and that they are valued. Parents should try hard to master the necessary matter-of-fact attitude.''

A child who knows about his or her body is more apt to be proud of it than one whose parents have been too embarrassed to discuss it. Such pride is important when a child reacts to an overly intimate touch by someone he or she knows. The child will then be able to say, ''Don't do that'' to whoever is bothering him or her. And Dr. Finkelhor adds, ''Kids who have self-esteem are less likely to be victimized.''

Sometimes parents are unwittingly insensitive to a child's feelings and reactions. For example, a mother may encourage a reluctant six-year-old to kiss everyone at a dinner party or to humor Uncle Louis who always wants an extra kiss or a cuddle. Children should not be exploited in ways that make expressions of fondness a meaningless exercise. And when they are repeatedly pressured to behave this way in social situations, they may lose a sense of certainty about their own feelings and responses. They can become confused and submissive.

Parents should always state clearly that it is all right for a child to object to some adult behavior. Even young children need to learn to trust their instincts. They should know, for example, that not all grownups have the privilege of kissing them and that everyone, no matter how small, can say no. Caresses are usually considered by a child as simple gestures of affection. But children should not be afraid to object strongly if anyone, known or unknown to them, tries to become more intimate than they want.

Children should be told this concept using simple and plain language, without sexual overtones. No one should embrace or caress another person who does not want to be touched. The child who objects is entirely right in spite of the fact that the aggressor is an adult, a member of the group children have been normally told to obey.

Moreover, experts point out that simple verbal objections made by a child can sometimes be an important defense against attempted molestation. A man who makes sexual advances to a small child may even be attracted by his intended victim's fear or compliance. A potential abuser may be effectively warded off by a child who can say, "Don't do that" or "I'll tell my mother."

"When children find out it is OK to tell an adult offender NO, they do," says Teri Poppino, director of the Sexual Assault Prevention Program for the Portland (Oregon) Police Bureau. "Most of the time, 80 to 90 percent, the adult offender stops. He is looking for an easy target, one that will keep quiet. The adult does not want to be found out."

Children should feel free to complain about adult behavior which they sense to be strange or repulsive to them no matter where and when it happens. The importance of this is illustrated by the following story told by a friend: When a pediatrician examined his preadolescent daughter to see if breast tissue was developing, he pinched her nipples. She felt abused and came home and told her parents. "That was the last time he saw her," her father told me.

I commented on how well my friend had handled the situation. His daughter had come home furious, saying, "Dr. so-and-so is a pervert." The parents took prompt and effective action. They realized that from then on she would have felt uncomfortable every time she saw this pediatrician because of his insensitivity. They found her a new doctor right away. In this family, communication about sexual matters was open and direct.

Had the father ever thought of confronting the doctor? He did not believe the situation warranted it. His daughter's description made it clear that the doctor's behavior was inappropriate and clumsy, but there was really nothing suspect.

The important thing was that this was a father who listened to his daughter's complaint and protected her. But he did not overreact and confront the pediatrician. Simply removing his daughter from the situation was enough. There are many times when a child's dignity can be affronted by a rather ordinary event.

In more serious cases, children should be told that some adults do not always behave like adults because they have problems and that it is best to avoid such people, not even to speak to them. But you should also stress that these are sad exceptions and that most people can be trusted; that there are other adults—teachers, school nurses, neighbors—to whom children can turn for help in a parent's absence.

Always bear in mind that the approach and tone you take toward molestation should be the same as in discussing crime; emphasize safety and what the child can do for self-protection. By talking in terms of safety measures, you will stress the positive. You should encourage your child freely to express fears, so you can discuss them calmly together. Always consider your particular child's personality. What you can say to one child in one way might be better said in a different way to another.

The process of establishing enough trust so a child will confide is the only reliable way to discover any troubling relationships that a child may be having with an acquaintance or someone in the family. The best preventive measure against child molesters who are not strangers is your own close rapport with your child.

There is no definite way to predict who among persons known to a child might commit a sexual offense. But you can lessen your children's chances of being molested by a friend, neighbor or relative by teaching them to respect their bodies, by telling them that it is all right to say no to what seems improper or repulsive to them and by establishing good communication within the family.

# ■ 8 ■

# Dealing with Child Molesters: Before and After

REPORTS of the sexual mistreatment of children have been growing, according to the National Center for the Prevention and Treatment of Child Abuse and Neglect. Estimates by child-protection organizations of how many American children are sexually abused each year range from 100,000 to 1,000,000, and many incidents go unreported. The Federal Bureau of Investigation estimates that only one in five of all sexual assaults are reported. And where children are concerned, incidents are usually reported only when hospitals or other social agencies are involved.

"The dimensions of the abuse are staggering," says Dr. A. Nicholas Groth, director of the sex-offender program at the Connecticut Correctional Institution in Somers, who has studied more than 1,000 child molesters since 1966. "All estimates are conservative. If we saw these same numbers of children suddenly developing some kind of illness, we'd think we had a major epidemic on our hands."

"For the most part parents have told their children to stay away from men who are wearing raincoats and carrying candy," says Dr. Gene G. Abel, director of the Sexual Behavior Clinic of the New York State Psychiatric Institute at the Columbia-Presbyterian Medical Center in Manhattan. "But none of our patients wear raincoats and carry candy. They come from all walks of life and all socio-economic categories, and they look just like the neighbor next door."

The Sexual Behavior Clinic is studying the behavior and treatment of child molesters. "What we have is a relatively small number of people committing a very large number of crimes," Dr. Abel says. "These offenders molest many more children than has been previously suspected and child molestation is a more frequent and serious crime than we had supposed."

Approximately one-third of all reported child molestation cases are committed by strangers, Dr. Abel says. Another third of the instances involve acquaintances known to the child—a neighbor, friend of the family or community figure—and one-third of the molestations are committed by primary relatives. Incest can involve stepchildren, sons and daughters, a younger sister or brother, a niece or nephew, or any child living in the offender's home in a non-marital situation.

Even though it is generally believed that girls are molested more often than boys, boys are as much at risk as girls, according to those who are studying the problem. Dr. Abel says that evidence from the last seven years of his studies shows that boys were more frequently victimized than girls. Other researchers state that the molestation of girls is more often reported. Boys are more hesitant to report because the molester is usually a man, and it involves the shame of a homosexual encounter.

Although the threat of sexual molestation by a stranger is a less frequent problem than that posed by someone known to the child, it is nevertheless a serious one, especially since it is often accompanied by abduction and violence.

When you talk to children about how to deal with strangers, you are trying to teach them appropriate responses and a useful set of skills to show them the safest course under specific circumstances. Children should also gradually be learning the difference between a situation that requires mere caution and one that calls for action on their part.

Remember the analogy of the fire drill. You want to teach a child to be prepared to take the safest actions in a particular situation. The emphasis should be on anticipation and prevention. If a child should ask what to do in case of a fire, you would explain in the simplest, most matter-of-fact way. You should do the same if a child asks what a stranger might do. There is no need to go into minute detail. You can say, "There are some strangers who hurt children, and we don't want that to happen to you." Many children have heard about sexual abuse from television. In that case, a TV program may offer a good opening for your talks. Again, remember that a straightforward, low-key approach will probably be less frightening than what children may have imagined or heard from their friends.

An important point for parents to remember about child molestation is that unhappy children can be the most vulnerable. Those who succumb without force are often influenced by a combination of soft-talking and bribery because they are lonely or neglected.

"Children aged eight to twelve who feel they have no allies are in a high-risk group," says Dr. Groth. He reports that a convicted offender, when asked how he picked his child victims, answered: "I would look at a schoolyard and find the child who was standing alone. The child who had thin clothes in winter. The child who was not as clean because the parents weren't taking good care of him."

Dr. Groth adds that "children are taught to cooperate

with adults and a child can cooperate without consenting.''
He believes that molesters capitalize on the vulnerability of
children, particularly "children who are feeling unwanted."

The finding that unhappy youngsters are most vulnerable
is supported by Dr. Martin Gipson who, with his colleagues
at the University of the Pacific, has developed a school program to prevent child molestation and abduction by strangers. Child victims, they found, had often been deprived of
parental attention or material things. These children will
consequently be more easily tempted by offers of money,
favors or other adult overtures.

There are many ways parents can help reduce the chances
that their children will become victims, not only by teaching
them how to act, but also by providing sufficient love and
attention at home. Part of caring for children is providing
appropriate supervision when a child is too young to venture
out of the house alone. It means knowing how much supervision is right for your child's age and personality. It also
means knowing how much your children really know, without deluding yourself into thinking they know more than
they actually do, and making sure they can handle themselves in situations to which they may be exposed.

Dr. Gipson and his colleagues believe that the best form
of prevention may be one which focuses on the circumstances characteristic of molestation incidents and teaches
children safe and sensible responses if they are caught in an
unhappy encounter. Children should learn how to act when
faced by a potential abductor or molester. While most parents tell their children to stay away from strangers, Dr.
Gipson's study found that children frequently have no real
idea of what they should actually do when, for example, a
friendly stranger asks them to go with him in a car. This innocence came to light when Dr. Gipson tested a method of
teaching children how to respond appropriately to suspicious advances by strangers. The program consisted of

slides and tapes which realistically portrayed ways in which child molesters have been known to approach their prey.

Dr. Gipson showed the particular segments to 368 elementary school children in Empire, California, a suburb of Modesto. The study involved the entire school of 15 classes, including seven from kindergarten through second grade and eight from third grade through fifth.

"Most children," he found, "are taught at a very young age that they 'don't talk to strangers' or 'don't take candy from a stranger.' However, they are not taught how to tell when a person may be classified as a stranger or whether or not other circumstances, such as helping a stranger look for a lost dog, are OK."

After the children viewed each situation, Gipson and his associates read them five possible responses. They were told to pick the one which they thought they would follow. The preferred response was to ignore the stranger and walk away. Five- to eight-year-olds gave that and other "correct" responses in only 13 of the 31 situations.

Younger children chose the more dangerous, inappropriate responses more often than did the older children, ages eight to ten. They also tended to be much more susceptible to a stranger's invitation to go home, to go for a ride or simply to join him to take a look at something. The younger children also were much more likely to give in to a stranger requesting something that did not involve money.

Among the kindergarten, first and second grade children, several said that they would cooperate with the stranger outright in every situation. They were easily tempted by offers of gifts or of something fun to do. In three specific situations the younger children responded dangerously by readily cooperating. One sample situation was enacted at a park bathroom, with a man saying, "Come over here, I want to show you something." Another showed a man asking help in finding a lost dog. In the third instance, a man says, "Do you like this kitten? Come to my house and I'll let you pick one out.''

The older children were more cautious, giving the safest answer in 25 out of the 31 situations. They were most susceptible to offers of money and to being told that other children had reacted in a certain way. On the whole, girls were more likely than boys to say that they would ignore a stranger (72 percent versus 40 percent). In many situations, boys were more likely than girls to say they really did not know what to do.

As they get older, children must be taught the more difficult choices they may have to make. Dr. Gipson's program aims at teaching children how to discriminate between different situations. These may involve an incident that requires some action on the child's part, such as running away; or it may only require that the child be careful. In such cases children learn by practicing suitable reactions.

The situations described in the ''pretend'' exercises which follow are adapted for parents to use at home from Dr. Gipson's program, which realistically portrays ways in which child molesters make their approaches. The lures depicted are those that actual child molesters have used with unsuspecting children. Even though not every potential situation can be described, the exercise gives children some specific cases to teach them how to handle themselves.

When you use such examples in your own talks with your children, you should always emphasize that not all strangers are bad and not all situations a child encounters will be dangerous. Your goal is to teach children how to tell the difference between encounters which merely require caution and others that call for action.

In your talks, you may notice that your child's answers though acceptable, may yet not be as safe as you would like. Children may, for example, feel obligated to make some verbal response to a stranger, such as saying no, when it would be best to ignore the stranger altogether and walk away. (If this has become a pattern, you may be able to have them practice saying nothing and then walking away.)

Sometimes a child may give an inappropriate and wholly unsafe response. For example, some boys may feel that they could overpower a stranger if threatened. In such cases, stress the reality of the situation by pointing out the differences in size and strength between children and adults.

While doing these exercises, you may find that your children are eager to discuss situations involving strangers that they or their friends have actually encountered. Encourage such discussion; your child will learn a great deal. Wind up with a determination of what the safest response would have been in the case they described.

Especially with young children, do not worry about repetition. You really want your child to get a firm grasp on things; to "overlearn" is the safest preparation for meeting potentially dangerous situations. The format may seem repetitious, but the aim is to teach how to react quickly and without hesitation.

The situations that follow can be added to the "What if" safety games you are already using. These examples can be introduced into family conversations. You can say, "Let's see what you would do if this happened." You may not want to offer your child all five alternatives at once, but select only a few.

If you have a preschool child and feel he or she is ready to start this program, you will probably not offer multiple choice answers. Instead, you can describe the situation and ask what the child would do. You may get an answer such as "I would be scared." Dr. Gipson suggests you look for an action-oriented response. Ask again, "When you get scared, what would you do?" If the child is having trouble, you can offer the answer. The next time you talk, see if your child remembers the example and your suggested response.

## Sample Situations Children May Encounter with Strangers †

**Preferred correct answer

*Acceptable answer

1. Pretend you are walking down the street, and a stranger comes up to you and asks you to go for a walk with him. Would you:
   (a) I don't know (b) Go with him (c) Ignore him and keep walking** (d) Say no* (e) Stop and talk to him.

2. What if the stranger offered you money to go with him? Would you:
   (a) Say no* (b) Stop and talk with him (c) I don't know (d) Go with him (e) Ignore him and keep walking.**

3. Pretend you are walking down the street, and a stranger comes up to you and asks you to go back to his house with him. Would you:
   (a) Ignore him and keep walking** (b) Stop and talk with him (c) Say no* (d) Go with him (e) I don't know.

4. Pretend you are walking down the street, and a stranger comes up to you and asks you to go for a ride in his car. Would you:
   (a) Go with him (b) Ignore him and keep walking** (c) I don't know (d) Stop and talk with him (e) Say no.*

5. Pretend you are walking down the street, and a stranger comes up to you and tells you that he will buy you something you want if you go to the store with him. Would you:

(a) Stop and talk with him (b) Go with him (c) Say no* (d) Ignore him and keep walking** (e) I don't know.

6. What if a stranger offered you money or something nice to get into his car? Would you:
   (a) Say no* (b) Stop and talk with him (c) Go with him (d) Ignore him and keep walking** (e) I don't know.

7. Pretend you are outside and a man in a car stops near you holding a kitten so you can see it. He says, "Do you like this kitten? Come to my house, and I'll let you pick one out." Would you:
   (a) Say, "Yes! I'd like a kitten." (b) Say, "No, thank you" and walk away* (c) Go to his house (d) Ignore him and walk away** (e) I don't know.

8. Pretend you are walking down the street, and a stranger in a car stops and asks for directions. Would you:
   (a) Give him the wrong directions on purpose (b) Ignore him and keep walking* (c) Tell him to ask someone else* (d) Stand back, tell him the directions if you know them and walk away** (e) I don't know.

9. What if the stranger offered you money or something nice to get in his car and show him the way? Would you:
   (a) Say no and walk away* (b) Get into his car if you knew the way (c) Ignore him and walk away** (d) Ask him how much money (e) I don't know.

10. Pretend you are outside playing when a man in a car with lots of dolls stops and says, "Hi, would

you like to go for a ride with these dolls?"
Would you:
(a) Say, "No, thank you" and walk away* (b) Ignore him and walk away** (c) Ask to look at the dolls (d) Say, "Yes, I would" (e) I don't know.

11. Pretend you are at a park and have to use the bathroom. A man standing near the door says to you, "Come over here. I want to show you something." Would you:
(a) Walk over to him (b) I don't know (c) Ignore him and go into the bathroom (d) Go back and tell your friends or parents** (e) Tell him, "Go away. You're bothering me."

12. Pretend you are outside and you see a man who says, "Hi, my dog just had some puppies. Would you like to see them?" Would you:
(a) Say yes (b) Say, "I have to ask my parents first" and walk away* (c) Ignore him and walk away** (d) I don't know (e) Say, "Yes, but just for a minute."

13. Pretend you are walking down the street, and you notice a stranger following you on foot. Would you:
(a) Walk back toward the man (b) Run away* (c) Let the man catch up with you and ask him if he is following you (d) Keep walking and go toward where there are other people** (e) I don't know.

14. Pretend you are outside when a man with a bag of cookies stops next to you in his car and says, "How'd you like something good to eat? These cookies are delicious." Would you:
(a) Say, "Yes, but just one." (b) Say, "No thank you" and walk away* (c) Say, "Yeah, I'm really

hungry." (d) I don't know (e) Ignore him and walk away.**

15. Pretend you are outside when a man holding a cat pulls up in his car and says, "Hey, somebody just took all my cat's kittens. Jump in my car and help me find them." Would you:
(a) Say, "No, I can't go with you without my parents."* (b) Say, "If we find them, can I have one?" (c) I don't know (d) Say, "Just for a little while." (e) Ignore him and walk away.**

16. Pretend you are playing in the park when a man walks up to you and says, "Please help me find my dog. He's run away and I can't find him." Would you:
(a) Ignore him and go tell your friends or parents** (b) Say, "Yes! But just for five minutes" (c) Say, "What does he look like? Maybe I've seen him." (d) Say, "No, I can't" and go tell your friends or parents* (e) I don't know.

†These incidents are selected from those used by Dr. Martin Gipson and his associates in the program Safety with Strangers. The examples are based on situations that actual child molesters used to attract children.

In spite of all precautions and the teaching of preventive measures, your child may actually experience sexual molestation. It can be anything from attempts to fondle the genitals to actual penetration. Whatever the type or the extent of the violation, it will be extremely upsetting to both your child and you.

The child should have been taught to report the molestation fully. Psychologist Steven Levenkron comments, "No one, child or adult, can be truly prepared for the violation of mind and body that takes place in a sexual assault. But children can be given the language which will enable them to relate the experience and to express their feelings about it.

Inability to do this has led to a great deal of persistent misery—lasting, in some cases I have seen, into the person's teens, 20s and 30s.

"I've worked with women who were molested as children by people they knew, such as building superintendents and stepfathers. I believe children can develop an enormous sense of responsibility for the molestation. Children often feel that they controlled the adult, that there was something about their behavior that caused it.

"The damage that I see, particularly in the women who blame themselves for what has happened to them, is enormous. I am thinking specifically of a woman who explained to me how her girlfriend's brother molested her at the age of six. She pretended she was asleep through the whole thing. And at the age of 30 she was still suffering from the bad memories. She had been calling herself a whore, in effect, since she had become old enough to realize what had happened. She had a very difficult time expressing this in therapy."

Levenkron believes that is typical of what happens. The child takes the blame and conceals the act. The longer no one knows, the more self-esteem is lost and the more suspicious the child is of himself or herself. That creates the long-term damage.

The short-term damage can be repaired, if there is language to express the experience. Parents can be sympathetic and not look at their child as if he or she is now damaged property. Given proper support, the child recovers and remembers the incident as an unpleasant experience, not as a traumatic one, unless the style of the molestation was traumatic.

Without hesitation a child should be able to report that "a man was walking around with his penis hanging out" or that "someone tried to touch my vagina." If a child does not know the right words or a parent has made the youngster feel that certain parts of the body are unmentionable, then there can be no communication about what happened or any alleviation of distress.

A child who has been sexually molested, whether or not there has been actual rape or physical harm, has lived through a frightening and perhaps incomprehensible experience. And for a parent to expect to remain calm under these circumstances is expecting the impossible. Finding out that your child has been victimized in this way can be overwhelming.

In this situation parents must cope with their own feelings of rage toward the perpetrator and probably also with some irrational guilt for their failure to protect the child. There must, however, be no room left for a mistake in the child's mind that he or she is the target of the parent's anger. If parents inadvertently give the impression that their rage is directed toward the child, the child can even be made to feel like the perpetrator. If parents communicate their own feelings of guilt, a child may feel insecure and confused.

## If You Suspect Your Child Has Been Molested

1. Do not blame or punish your child for the actions of others.
2. Do not create the impression that he or she has done something "bad."
3. Provide assurance of your support, love and concern.
4. Take time to listen. Do not dismiss what your child tells you as exaggeration or a figment of the imagination.
5. Take positive steps when necessary. Report the incident, if this is appropriate.

The child has been embarrassed at the least, probably humiliated and possibly physically overpowered. He or she may wonder if some weakness on his or her part was responsible for what happened. After all, children often believe that pleasant experiences are the result of their good behavior; it is only natural that they should blame unpleasant ones in their minds on their own misbehavior or some violation of the adult world's complex rules. The most well-known example is children's frequent belief that they are responsible for their bad behavior. Similarly, a child who has been sexually molested may feel that she has somehow caused the indignity.

How can parents help children avoid permanent emotional trauma in the wake of sexual molestation? Should the child be rushed to a psychiatrist or a psychologist?

Therapy is not automatically indicated, most experts feel. Steven Levenkron believes that the parents may benefit from talking to someone else before attempting to comfort their child. Parents need to unburden themselves of their feelings about the situation, both for their emotional well-being and also to find the right words to comfort their child. It is often the parents who will be most helped by discussing their feelings and reactions with a trusted professional. The person can be a psychiatrist or anyone else the parents trust who is qualified—a physician, minister, psychologist or any other trained person involved in dealing with interpersonal problems.

Only after they feel ready to communicate without letting their own rage and guilt interfere, should parents gently try to get a full report from the child—encourage talk about the incident, but without pressure. You can say something, such as "When you feel like talking, we are here to listen. We want to help you."

It is important not to grill a child, but to listen carefully and show nonhysterical concern. You may encourage a child to remember details—and describe the offender—without demanding quick answers.

Remember that in most cases he or she has not been suddenly or violently attacked. Usually, there has been some kind of friendly overture. Only later did what may have started as casual touching or a playful game turn into aggression. It is very natural for the child to be confused. When you are talking about it afterward, you can add that you would like to find the molester in order to prevent him from scaring and hurting other children.

Short-term discomfort experienced by children while they are getting over a distressing incident need not be cause for further concern unless it persists. The child may have nightmares about the incident—a common reaction. Ordinarily, the bad dreams will diminish and then disappear in due time. While they last, parents can comfort the child by saying that "scary things that are bothering you sometimes come out at night instead of in the daytime," but also by predicting that the bad dreams will go away.

In addition, parents should not be seriously worried if for a while a child does not want to go to a particular place or if there is some sensitivity associated with the body part that has been molested. Even if there has been no physical injury, a child may feel awkward about touching the sensitive area or having anyone else touch it. Your response should be sympathetic and tactful, perhaps expressed in a simple acknowledgment, such as, "I guess you feel uncomfortable." You will want to reassure the child that these feelings will pass and that there has been no lasting harm.

How parents can help is illustrated by one ugly incident. A 10-year-old girl had been molested by a delivery man who regularly brought groceries to her home and was well liked by the family. One day they were shocked to learn that this delivery man had forced his penis into the girl's mouth. They took legal action to have the man prosecuted; but their primary concern was to minimize the emotional damage to their daughter. Professional counseling helped her deal with her reactions to the incident. Most important though, the parents worked hard to restore their daughter's sense of self-worth. The mother said wisely: "What I was more concerned about was that she know she was a good girl. She did nothing wrong. He did something wrong. I just try to impress on her that I still love her. I was heartbroken that something like this happened to her, but it did; so where was I going to go from there? I was going to give her as much support and love as I could.''

By reassuring her daughter that not everyone behaves like that, the mother hoped to rebuild her daughter's trust in people, which had been undermined by a tragic encounter with someone she had once trusted. The mother told her daughter, ''It's too bad that there are things like this in our society, but you have to deal with it.''

The parents were also quite understandably worried about the possible effect the experience might have on the girl's future attitudes toward sex. They wanted to reassure her that not all men were bad and that only a few sick ones would act in such a contemptible fashion. After a while, the girl responded to their reassurances, reinforced by affection. The memories continued to surface from time to time, but she was less and less frightened and gradually became more comfortable with male friends of the family.

In general, a child should be reassured that the frightening experience is a thing of the past, that it will not happen again and that she is now safe and surrounded by people who love and understand her. Gradually, she will forget and feel better.

If disturbing aftereffects continue for longer than a month, or if the child's behavior changes radically, there may be a more serious problem. If, for example, a child remains afraid to go out and play or the nightmares persist or there is changed behavior at school or at home, then professional help is probably called for. (See Chapter 7.)

Finally, Steven Levenkron suggests that a girl who has been raped in childhood, even if all seems well afterward, should have the benefit of preventive therapy before the onset of adolescence. Such emotional insurance aims at avoiding further complications of the normally turbulent teen years by a distorted attitude resulting from a frightening earlier experience. "Counseling at this crucial time can resolve conflicts and help to assure that the girl's future emotional and sexual relationships will be healthy and happy."

In the case of physical injury or rape, the parent's first priority is to consult a physician. This should be done whether or not the injury involves the genitals. If possible, a doctor already known to the child should be consulted. A girl or a boy can be taken to their regular pediatrician or family physician. For a girl, her mother's gynecologist may be a good choice. In the event that no known doctor is available, you can take a child to a hospital emergency room.

Whatever medical help you receive, a parent—preferably of the same sex—should stay with a child during any examination and during treatment if it is needed. Remember that a good medical check-up can be reassuring to a child. Whenever possible a child will benefit from being prepared beforehand to see a doctor. Sometimes children feel that a medical examination is like a test they will either "pass" or "fail." This is the time for a parent to restore the child's confidence and say he or she is fine. The doctor is testing for certain particular things; the examination is in no way a judgment of the child's worth or goodness.

Levenkron adds, "Be sure the child understands what's happening during an examination of the genital or rectal area. You can say, 'The doctor is checking to make sure that everything is OK.' If there is any physical damage to be mended, a parent should give a reassuring but honest and realistic explanation of what to expect." If there is going to be any pain, be open and direct, saying something such as, "This may hurt" or "You may be somewhat uncomfortable for a while, but it will be better very soon."

* * *

The need to educate parents in handling incidents of sexual abuse was noted in the comprehensive Boston Study of Child Abuse, conducted by Dr. David Finkelhor. (See Chapter 8.) Only slightly more than half of the families involved reported the abuse to any outside agency. Among those not reporting, there was a strong feeling that the episode was no one else's business—they could handle it themselves.

Of those parents who did report the incident, 74 percent went to the police rather than to social agencies. Such reporting, it seemed to Dr. Finkelhor, was mainly motivated by the parents' desire to punish the offender and perhaps protect other children from a similar fate. But parents should be aware that child molestation is, regrettably, often treated more leniently than most other major crimes. According to Professor Irving Prager of the LaVerne College of Law, throughout the United States, less than 10 percent of convicted felony child molesters go to prison.

Whether or not to report sexual molestation to the police can be a more difficult decision than whether to report a mugging. It is up to the parent to consider the particular circumstances, always putting the child's best interests first. Your decision ultimately will undoubtedly be based in part on your estimate of how the authorities in your area will react.

Oregon, for example, offers the choice of reporting either to the local law enforcement agency or to the Children's Services Division. A social worker and a detective will usually be assigned to the case. The caseworker will also help with counseling child and family.

Once the investigation is completed, the case is turned over to the district attorney's office for review and to decide whether prosecution is in order. That decision is ultimately made by the deputy district attorney, but the parent's feelings and involvement are given due consideration.

If the case does go to trial, the judge will usually set a

time to speak with the child to be sure that he or she understands the difference between right and wrong (between the truth and a lie) and also to make it easier to be a witness in the courtroom. (The competency hearing takes place in many states. But now in a number of states the trend has been to abolish such provisions and adopt the rules of evidence that children can be witnesses without any prior attempt to determine their competence, according to the American Bar Association's National Legal Resource Center for Child Advocacy and Protection in Washington, D.C.)

In cases of very young children, the judge tells each attorney to treat the victim with respect and sensitivity and to ask questions as gently as possible. The Oregon booklet "Touch That Hurts" tells parents that there will be times throughout the process when they will feel "just tired of the whole thing." No attempt is made to minimize the difficulties for either parents or children. The authors suggest that if the situation begins to feel even slightly out of control, parents can take advantage of the counselors available in their communities who are there to help.

"Parents did not spontaneously mention child protection or mental health agencies or physicians as possible sources of assistance in our study," says Dr. Finkelhor. Although they did not state strong anxieties about what would happen if they did report the abuse, they were probably not aware of some of the potential benefits of professional help. Very few parents consulted doctors, mental health or child protection agencies. They did not seem to have much interest in consulting someone who might help assure a child's well-being. In fact, Dr. Finkelhor reports that parents in the study did not express much concern about the child's well-being. He believes they were either covering up their feelings or they had such faith in their children's resiliency that they saw no real cause for concern.

Frequently, Dr. Finkelhor observes, parents do not know that other professionals beside the police might be called upon for help. When parents learn about the work of these agencies, they acknowledge them as valuable sources of comfort. For parents to know there are many sources of help in the community is one important step toward making sure that in the long run children will suffer less from childhood sexual victimization, and that there are effective and humane ways of healing a traumatic memory.

# ◼ 9 ◼

# Thieves, Gangs and Bullies in School

A FEW years ago in Austin, Texas, a 14-year-old boy stood before horrified classmates and shot a teacher to death. More recently in Long Island, a disturbed former school maintenance worker, still in his teens, held a junior high class hostage after he had shot the principal; he then killed himself. All parents react with horror to spectacular front-page stories about violence in our schools.

Fortunately, such events, while widely publicized, are rare. What is much more frequent and troubling than the occasional outrage committed by psychopaths is the prevalence of theft and robbery in the schools. According to a study by the National Institute of Education (NIE), 11 percent, or 2.4 million, of all American secondary school children have something worth more than $1 stolen from them during any given month. Most of the reported thefts involve small amounts of money, sweaters, books, notebooks and other property commonly found in lockers. Only one-fifth of the reported losses involved money or property worth $10 or more.

Petty theft in schools appears to be commonplace every-where, usually beginning in seventh grade. Ed Muir of the United Federation of Teachers, says that in many public schools, "kids are in danger in the schoolyards, the corri-dors, the bathrooms and the lunchrooms. Even on their way to school, some kids have to worry about people—and other kids—who want to take their bus passes, their money, their book bags or their jackets." (See Chapter 5.)

Experts agree that school safety problems are a product of the society in which we live. Schools reflect the outside world—its values as well as its frustrations—and inequities spill over into the schools.

Many observers believe that students, particularly in large, overcrowded schools, tend to feel neglected and lost. In classes with too many students, it is difficult to develop close relationships either with a teacher or other pupils. Cor-ridors are often crowded, particularly when classes change. So are cafeterias. They can resemble mob scenes. Student alienation often develops in an impersonal school setting.

And unfortunately, many schools are large. It is less ex-pensive to build large buildings, school boards have found. Many high schools are packed with 3,000 or more students.

Another factor causing student safety problems is that in recent years a sluggish economy has forced school budgets to be slashed. As a result, classes have gotten larger as schools have been closed and teachers laid off. In many areas, the result has been more pressures on both teachers and students. Moreover, many special services have been cut out and extracurricular activities eliminated.

An estimated 1.3 percent, about 282,000, secondary stu-dents, report that they have been attacked in school during a typical one-month period, according to the NIE study. The proportion of junior high school students reporting was about twice that of senior high school students (2.1 versus 1 percent). About two-fifths of the reported attacks resulted in some injury, but only a fraction (4 percent) involved injuries serious enough for medical attention. The risk of a minor attack is about the same everywhere, but serious attacks are most frequent in big-city schools.

Incidents of personal violence, theft and disruptive acts in the schools were found to occur mostly during regular school hours and more frequently in the middle of the week. Within schools, classrooms are the safest places, the NIE study found. The areas of highest risk are corridors and stairs between classes. Restrooms, cafeterias, locker rooms and gyms also pose considerable safety risks.

The great majority of all reported in-school offenses were committed by current students. In most attacks and robberies, the offender is recognized by the victim. With few exceptions, the chances of being a victim of either attack or robbery in secondary schools declines steadily as grade level increases. Seventh graders are most likely to be attacked or robbed; 12th graders least likely.

Violence is more prevalent in schools where the enrollment is less than 40 percent white. However, the NIE research showed that there is no relation between a school's racial and ethnic make-up and the incidence of violence if other factors, such as the amount of crime in the neighborhood, are taken into account: "The more crime and violence students are exposed to outside school, the greater the problems in school." In addition, the presence of young nonstudents around the school increases the risk.

Even when students themselves are not personally involved in an unpleasant incident, just hearing about or witnessing such events can be a troubling experience. Tara Reinhart of Fairfax, Virginia, saw a fight in her high school:

*Two boys were nearly killing each other—fighting harder than I've ever seen two people fight. When someone finally pulled them apart, their faces were puffy and bleeding. Any-*

*one who'd witnessed the fight (and plenty of people did) was
jumpy for the rest of the day. I can still hear the sound; the
dull thud between face and fist.*

*I don't know why I'm so shook up. Except . . . I'd never
seen a fight like this. . . . This was real. I could see pain
from each blow. I could almost feel it. . . .*

While a majority of attacks and robberies in school involve victims and offenders of the same race, a "substantial
proportion" is interracial—42 percent of the attacks and 46
percent of the robberies. "For minority students the risks
are higher in predominantly white schools (70 percent or
more white): for white students, the risks are greater in minority schools." School and class size are crucial. "It seems
that when teachers and administrators can establish personal
relationships with students, the risks of violence decrease,"
the NIE report says.

Despite the report's gloomy facts and statistics, many
children attend school safely. And many schools have found
ways of reducing risks and averting violence.

The Charlottesville–Albermarle County School District is
an example of a school system that promotes safety and pre-
vents crime through a part of the curriculum called TIPS
(Teaching Individual Protective Strategies). To help stem
the rising tide of crimes committed both against juveniles
and by them, the Federal Bureau of Investigation invited the
Virginia school district to develop a pilot program of crime
prevention which could be used in schools everywhere. The
goals: to teach children to respect other people's opinions
and property; to help solve everyday conflicts without violence; and to teach ways in which students could actively
prevent crime.

By working with community groups as well as educators,
TIPS has developed various classroom activities for students at

each elementary grade level. For example, there are teacher-led discussions on how common classroom disagreements might be settled without fighting; there are worksheets with games and puzzles that explain how students can respond to certain situations such as attacks by bullies and there are role-playing exercises and case studies to teach students how a victim might have avoided a particular incident.

"It's important to build safety awareness early," says Loreli Damron, the project director. "That's what makes it prevention instead of correction or heightened vulnerability. We are teaching positive solutions to conflict and how to deal with it using rules and law. It's part of our curriculum."

Parents support the program objectives by helping children with their exercises at home. TIPS begins in kindergarten and goes up to eighth grade, providing systematic and sequential teaching units designed to foster constructive behavior. The program can be used by classroom teachers or volunteers and requires no special equipment or expanded facilities. The materials are not expensive, and the program blends easily into a school's regular curriculum.

In another program in Pittsburgh, school officials felt that it was essential to involve students in maintaining a safe environment. A student security aide program, instituted by the local Board of Education, has students working with the security staff to maintain order and safety.

Started in 1973 to ease racial tensions, the program has grown to include 1,100 students during the 1982–83 school year. It operates on the premise that there is a "magic configuration of influence kids have over their peers," says Stanley Rideout, chief of security for the Pittsburgh schools. "We got a congress of student council members and delinquent bad kids to work for the good of the schools and we turned them around." The unusual aspect of the program was to create a core of leaders in each school composed not only of student government representatives and class officers, but also of leaders of the school's most disruptive elements.

Stanley Rideout is the overall coordinator of the program. Each principal is responsible for the selection in his or her school of the staff security officers and teacher advisors. Students apply for patrol duty; the principal has the final word in the selection process.

While on duty, student aides wear special jackets representing the school colors. Their assignments include patroling the halls, lavatories, sports events and other extracurricular activities. Many of the schools have closed circuit television, monitored by students to spot potential trouble and to try to stop it before it gets out of hand. "We tell the kids the TV cameras are there to prevent vandalism, a positive reason," says Rideout.

Each school operates a training program which teaches the security aides how to solve problems without physical confrontation. They learn to talk to other students and to think of themselves as peace officers.

"In our program," Rideout adds, "kids persuade other kids to keep the school 'cool.' " In the 1982–83 school year, there was less vandalism than at any previous time. In addition, peace has been established between blacks and whites, and the in-school theft rate is low.

"We were first brought in to calm race riots in the school. They were terrible. Since then, we haven't had any serious disruption. We have time to concentrate on crime against individuals. We have gained the expertise to do preventive work instead of just putting out fires."

In other examples of efforts to improve school safety by involving students, Dallas and Colorado Springs have turned to local citizen's groups. In the late 1970s, community groups, police and concerned parents got together to deal with the escalation of violence. "It works when people get together to solve problems," says Phil King of the National Education Association. While some difficulties will still exist, they will not be nearly as frequent or widespread.

"What astounds me," says Ed Muir, "is how little trouble there is in the large schools I have observed. The potential for nasty scenes is always there. Yet, in many places students and teachers manage to live together because they don't let little incidents build up and they don't let anything big happen. Often, groups work out rules among themselves."

A key to school safety is the creation of personal relationships which give students, teachers and administrators a sense of community and identity. Particularly in an integrated school with different racial and ethnic groups, Ed Muir stresses it is vital for children to get to know youngsters from groups other than their own on a first-name basis. Once you are known as an individual, you are less likely to be attacked or ripped off, even in a setting where occasional hostilities or suspicions may persist. Groups seek out the unknown "Whitey" or "Blackie" as a victim. If you are Harry or Bill, your personal identity overshadows any racial classification.

"One thing that helps make you a target is anonymity," says Muir. "So get to know different groups—for two reasons. First, to avoid getting ripped off or involved in a fight. Second, if you know members of another group personally and by name, they know you can identify them to the authorities if there is any trouble. That can be a protection."

In some schools, there is gang activity. Gang members may extort money. It is hard to advise children about what to do, Muir says, except to tell them to avoid the situation in the first place. If this proves impossible, parents must assess the particular case. Your child may not even tell you, but cover up by saying something like, "I need money for a review book."

As an example, a high school student I will call Peter did

not confide in his parents about gang activity at his school.
The parents suspected a problem, but Peter volunteered no
specific information. His parents never figured out there
was any relation between the school gang's activity and the
fact that every day at noon Peter came home for a few minutes. He had already had his lunch. He would say only that
he had forgotten something he needed for class. Later, his
parents learned that he had been coming home to use the
bathroom. In school it had become the place for liquor and
drugs, and he was afraid to enter. It was his way of dealing
with a troublesome situation without telling his parents—an
example of many children's fear of confiding in their families because they worry that what they told them might be
made public. Fear of retaliation can also keep a child silent.

For similar reasons it is often difficult to decide whether
to report to school authorities. What is absolutely essential is
that you consult your child's wishes in this matter, even if
you feel that, eventually, action should be taken. You
should assess the situation together. Ed Muir says, "Just
what school or police authorities can do to insure the protection of kids with school-related problems is often unclear.
There are no textbook answers. You have to ask yourself,
'How much power do they have?' and 'How serious is the
problem?' "

In some communities special arrangements are available
for parents together with their children to cope with a troubling episode. Pittsburgh, for example, has established procedures for young people to report thefts and extortions
without fear of retribution.

"Cases are handled by a meeting in my office," Stanley
Rideout says, "with parents and the high school principal. I
operate a quasi-judicial process to take care of complaints."
He states that he has not had any retaliation during the three
years he has been doing this. "I find that if students are encouraged to report violations, there is minimal reason for

fear. Those who are afraid to tell their parents or the school continue to be victimized. We can't solve problems we don't know about.

"Parents must know what happens in school," he says. "A kid must know he can come and tell a parent. The parent should help the student understand that the law is on their side."

Not all schools offer such procedures. Nor does every school enjoy the benefit of people who can be trusted by both parents and students. If parents sense a dangerous situation exists and—this is an important consideration—if they have confidence in the principal, they should talk to him or her privately, always with the firm understanding that their complaint remain anonymous. If this is difficult within the school, then an outside meeting with the principal or other schol representative ought to be arranged.

In any case if you are considering an approach of this kind, it may be best for several parents to join together, thus eliminating the suspicion that the problem is merely personal or atypical. In the case of a racially mixed school, such an informal presentation should be made jointly by parents from the different groups.

You can help your child recognize and deal with crime-related problems at school. Listen carefully to what children tell you and be on the lookout for the hidden aspects. Just the fact that your child is talking about a problem will often bring some relief. You can also offer some specific pointers about how to spot trouble and what situations to avoid:

- If there is more or less noise than usual among a group of other students.
- If other children are seen crowding together on a playground or on a corridor.
- If a child is "standing guard" at a bathroom door.

The chances are your child already knows a great deal about what signals when "something is in the air." He or she probably knows that when a particular group gets together there will most likely be trouble. And there are probably some kids who should be avoided at all times.

There are some other common-sense measures for your children to follow to minimize the dangers of getting ripped off. Many are things that they probably do now in school.

When changing clothes in a locker room, it is smart to keep a wallet or purse inside the locker, in a pocket or within sight close by. Never leave possessions lying out on open benches where you cannot see them. Valuables should never be left in desks that do not lock or in lockers that are not secure.

When washing up in a lavatory, do not take off rings and leave them on the sink within someone else's reach for easy picking. (Also you don't want to leave a ring on the edge of a sink because it can easily go down the drain.) In fact, you should warn your children never to wear valuable jewelry to school, including jewelry that may have sentimental value.

## What Can Parents Do to Help with School Safety?

1. Encourage your child to report to you any upsetting incidents. Discuss ways of dealing with problems, including going to the authorities together to decide on the best course.

2. See that your child does not get to school very early or stay too late, unless some adults are present. Suggest that children come to school and go home with friends.

3. Support the school's security rules and see that your child obeys them.

4. Try to become involved in your child's school, not only on safety issues, but in all areas of educational concern.

Ed Muir offers additional suggestions. First, try not to be alone in school or while walking to and from school. "When a child uses the bathroom, he or she should do it when everyone else is using it during a change of periods. A crowd is your best protection. The crazies stay away when there are a lot of people around."

Safety in numbers is a crucial message to get across. If your child is late or slow in changing clothes in the locker, tell him or her to ask a friend to stick around. Students who stay for an extracurricular activity will be safer if friends accompany them. In fact, having many friends is a good means of protection. Encourage your child to join in several different extracurricular activities; this is a good way to increase the number of other students he or she knows. It is not necessary to know children well in order for them to be part of a network. They will know each other by sight. Memberships in sports, clubs, student government or musical groups forms the basis for new friendships and widens your child's circle of acquaintances.

Ed Muir sees only a limited role for teachers in keeping children safe. "Most assaults on students are committed by other students—not in the presence of teachers. There is little that teachers can do about this, other than helping to improve their school's general atmosphere and overall safety pattern."

It is a good idea for children in school to ask others, particularly older students, what is and is not considered safe behavior. They should find out, for example, just who is going to the basketball game after school and plan to go along with them, and to go home with someone who lives in the same neighborhood.

Also, your child should wear the same kind of clothes everyone else is wearing, the unofficial school uniform. "You have to be a zebra in a herd of zebras," Ed Muir says, "not a gazelle. It is important for a child to blend in with other children and not to stand out as unusual in dress." Parents should not ridicule their children for wanting to dress like everyone else. On the contrary, they should encourage it. This is one case where you can't say "I don't care what the other kids wear. I want you to dress differently." You don't. And in addition, any sort of status symbols in dress, or a special radio, watch, gold chains, anything that makes a child stand out, is to be avoided.

## Coping with Bullies

The problem of the school bully is as old as school itself. How can a child, especially one in the early grades, confront a bully?

I remember when Paul, our older son, was in third grade, he once came home and told us that a boy called Steve told him not to play with a girl named Julie. If Paul ignored the order, Steve was going to beat him up. When I asked who Steve was, Paul told me he was a fourth grader and "very big." He told me he was scared.

As I put my arm around him, I told him that we would figure out a way to handle it. I said this with more confidence than I felt. While this was no "serious" threat of a gang extorting his lunch money, it was a problem all the same. How could I help?

There were many things I thought of telling Paul in my first upset moments. Since his day was generally supervised, I had assumed that he would never have to face a threatening situation. I was also angry and thought of the half-joking advice a friend had offered. "Tell him to kick the kid—where it hurts.'' Another mother had suggested that I call the principal. I even considered boxing or judo lessons.

After I had calmed down, I recognized that there were limits to what I, as a parent, could do. My help would have to be indirect. Paul would have to deal with the situation himself. He eventually did, through a combination of talking to Steve and explaining that Julie wanted to have lots of friends and also by asking another friend, Andy, who was big for his age, to come with him while he talked to Steve.

I was relieved that Paul had dealt with the situation and hoped that future encounters with bigger boys could be faced as successfully. I was especially glad I had not rushed in to see the principal. If I had, Paul would never have learned how to deal with things himself. Even though I recognized that his solution might not work the next time around, he and I were both proud that he had worked things out independently.

Our second son, John, had some problems with bullies on the school bus. He began to complain that he did not want to get on the bus, sometimes even wanting to stay home from school. We had some difficulty getting him to tell us what was wrong, but we said to him, ''Look, you haven't got a cold. Why do you want to stay home from school? Why all of a sudden is school no fun anymore?''

He was trying to avoid a potentially difficult situation, but it was hard for him to describe what was happening on the bus because, for the moment, much of the bullying was verbal. It was the kind of teasing that goes on between children. The older kids on his bus felt themselves in charge; the younger ones seemed to be taking turns being victims and joining the older tormentors. John was unsure about where he fitted in or when he might become the victim. He saw that children were always changing sides and he was confused.

We talked about how angry he felt confronted by all this. But by now I knew better than to offer to intercede right away. After our talk, John seemed more comfortable about facing the kids and handling the problem himself. The talking and the knowledge that we were available as a last resort seemed to comfort him.

We explained that children's attitudes change very quickly—who belongs to which group and who is getting picked on. He began to notice that this was true. We also told him that most children are as likely to be victims as often as they are aggressors, and that a lot of children "swing" from being on your side to being an attacker. They will take turns supporting you and joining cliques to bully you.

Children act like bullies for a variety of reasons. To understand why another child is turning to bullying can sometimes help your child cope. He or she can then see the bully as less omnipotent and threatening—just another youngster with problems.

"If your child can see the bully as someone whose parents are getting divorced or who has a big brother who beats him up regularly at home, you are taking the bully off the pedestal of awe where the child has placed him," says a New York psychologist. "Your child may then feel stronger in relationship to that youngster because he or she can see the bully himself as victim in another setting."

This new way of viewing a bully may encourage your child to challenge him or her instead of seeing the person as all-powerful. Children often picture bullies as omnipotent in their own minds as a way to justify their reluctance to challenge them. But if you can help them see the bully as someone who is getting beaten up at home, his or her power is soon deflated. Then your child can look more realistically at what had been a forbidding image and, in turn, rely more on his or her own strengths in dealing with the situation.

Seeing the bully in this new light should not be confused when asking your child to ''forgive,'' the psychologist adds. ''I don't think that is useful at all.'' Your child's anger is appropriate, and you want him or her to be able to mobilize that anger in finding the best way to handle a bully.

In that search, you can help your child in several ways. Be supportive. Don't brush off incidents, especially those against younger children, as trivial, even if they appear so to you. Confidence to deal with bullies comes only with experience. If you minimize an experience, you may hamper the development of self-confidence.

Watch how your child behaves after an episode; be sensitive to feelings and respond on that level. Sometimes your child will act braver than he or she feels. Do not be misled by any show of bravado. Children may feel great about the way they handled a particular situation. But they may have been terrified underneath. They may even tell you that the experience was ''not a big deal'' because they do not want to admit they were afraid. You can reduce this anxiety and make it all right for them to acknowledge their fears if you say, for example, ''If that happened to me, I would have been afraid.'' And don't forget your praise for handling the situation well.

Wait until a child is ready to confide in you. At that time, you may want to tell him about a bullying experience you once had. Be sure, however, that you do not dramatize your story in a way that might reawaken fears.

Despite the fact that physical confrontations and bullying happen more often to boys, girls should also learn to handle these kinds of situations.

Try to help put the bullying experience into perspective if your child seems overwhelmed by it. You can calm some fears by first coming up with specific ways to solve the problem. Then you can also reassure your child that he or she has the ability to carry out the plans successfully.

Your child's anxiety and discomfort will be reduced if you adopt a positive and confident attitude. Let a child know that there are many problems in life and that the idea is to gain a handle on dealing with them. When you offer a particular solution, try to assess its effectiveness with your child. You may have to state firmly that a strategy that worked in one situation may not work in a second incident. Many children are inclined to use the same solution to every problem or to let their fears dam up their thinking. That is why it is necessary to point out alternatives to them in your talks.

Don't suggest that children look to an older person—whether it is a teacher, parent, principal or big brother—for help in each threatening situation. Encourage a child to deal personally with the problem first. If, as a parent, you believe that you or someone else should intercede, ask your child how he or she feels about it. We were very surprised when we asked John if he would like us to intervene in his bus problem. He was emphatic in telling us to keep hands off.

Offer some suggestions on how to deal with particular situations. Present a diplomatic way first—trying to cope with a problem using words. But there are other options if talking fails to do the trick. To fight is one.

Your own attitudes about fighting will govern what you tell your children. We told our boys that they probably should not fight for something or about something unless it was really important to them. If it means a lot, fight for it; but don't fight for minor reasons. In the last analysis, whether or not a child fights is up to what he or she considers to be at stake. Children usually have a good idea of what they can do in a given situation without acting like a daredevil or a coward.

Flight is another alternative. There are times when it is appropriate to run away. Your child probably knows not to fight with anyone bigger. You can reassure your children by telling them that they are not being wimps by running away from a much bigger child. It is the smart thing to do. (See Chapter 5.)

Parents naturally want to protect their children from having bad experiences; but it is important to realize that there is a limit to what they can do. No matter how difficult it may be for us, the recognition that every frightening experience children can surmount, including being bullied or threatened, will ultimately help them to become more confident and independent, which in turn will improve their capacity to deal with whatever happens to them.

# ▣ 10 ▣

# Safety in Traffic and in Cars

Traffic has always been a hazard for children. Youngsters who live in urban areas must deal with it every day. Even in the suburbs, children whose residential street is not lined with parked cars must learn to watch out for the occasional speeding vehicle.

But the problem lies mainly in cities. Traffic accidents involving pedestrians are increasing. In New York City, for example, there were nearly 2,000 more traffic injuries and 6,000 more accidents in the first eight months of 1982 than during the same period a year earlier. These figures and similar ones in other cities worry parents as they wonder when to let their children cross streets alone for the first time. I remember hanging out of our sixth-floor apartment window watching our boys on their first such venture.

### Some Questions to Ask When You Are Considering Letting Children Cross the Street Alone:

1. Do they know where to cross the street?
2. Are there Walk/Don't Walk signs at every crossing? Can your child read them?
3. What is the job of the crossing guard (if your school has one)?
4. What does a stop sign mean?
5. Does your child know what a pedestrian is?

When to launch children on that independent journey is a complicated decision that depends on many things. There is no fixed age that is "right" for every child. One deciding factor should be the amount of traffic in your neighborhood and your estimate of how hazardous the streets are.

It should be comforting for parents to remember that they have been training children how to cross streets for years, using personal example. When you are with your children, you have always crossed on the green lights only and looked for cars in both directions. You have made a point of holding your child's hand. You concentrated on crossing and walking purposefully. Children learn by imitation. This is the best preparation you can offer.

When you are teaching traffic safety rules to your children, make sure they really understand what is involved. For example, children often assume that, if they can see a car, the driver can also see them. Explain that because of their size, children may be out of the driver's range of vision. Remind them that in some places the pedestrian does not have the right-of-way, and even where they do, the rule is more honored in its breach than its observance.

To find out what your child knows, ask questions. Can your child read the "Walk" and "Don't Walk" signs? Test out whether he or she actually looks first to the right, then to the left, then right again before crossing. Does your child know right and left automatically or does he or she have to think it over? Does your child know what the word "pedestrian" means?

Many excellent traffic education programs are offered in schools across the country. For example, a program for preschool through first grade called "Tony the Talking Traffic Light" is a popular one. It is distributed by the Southwest Texas State University, Institute of Criminal Justice. In this program, the traffic light "talks" to the children: "You know that my red light tells cars when to stop, and my green light means go, and my yellow light means slow down and be careful. Well, there are red light and green light people and things, too . . ."

Some simple lessons are offered: "A policeman does a lot of things in his daily job of protecting life and property. He watches homes and business places during the night so that you will all be safe. He finds lost children, and sometimes he finds lost parents, too. He helps firemen by directing traffic around fires before the firemen get there." But no matter how good a job your school is doing with traffic safety, you must still teach your own child about crossing the street.

Before you let a child cross alone, stage some rehearsals. Ask the child to decide when you both should cross. Frequent rehearsals will give you an idea of the child's actual understanding of traffic, not just what rules may have been memorized.

American parents can learn from European studies. At the Swedish Institute of Child Psychology, Dr. Stina Sandels analyzed in detail the complete police investigations of a sample of approximately 20 percent of that nation's traffic accidents during the late 1960s involving children aged one to ten.

Only the very young children, one and two years old, had been accompanied by adults. Detailed analysis of the accident records led Dr. Sandels to the conclusion that the adults supervising children displayed a lack of knowledge about what to expect from a child in dealing with traffic. They overestimated the children's ability to cope.

Only in a few cases had supervisors been negligent or were children hit by cars even though they had followed all the rules. In most instances, the children's inability to understand, and deal with, traffic had caused the accidents.

### Suggestions for Young Children in Traffic*

1. Do not cross streets without holding on to the child's hand.
2. Never let small children out of sight in the vicinity of parked cars or moving traffic.
3. Do not let two- or three-year-old children play in traffic-exposed areas alone or only in the company of other small children.
4. Do not rely on children—whom you've forbidden to cross the street or bicycle in traffic—to remember what you have told them.
5. Never make a child afraid of the police. Instead say that the policeman is willing and able to help him or her in traffic.
6. Never permit children to stand around and watch parked vehicles without your immediate supervision. They may run into the street and be hit by cars.
7. Do not allow children to ride their bicycles on roads with a great many cars until they are at least 12 years old.

*Adapted from Swedish Traffic Study

Another study concluded that due to limited perceptual ability and physical coordination, children below the age of nine could not deal with traffic competently. Even though curb drill can be mastered by rote memory, says Dr. Sandels, an international authority on the behavior of children in traffic, children do not really understand all they are told to memorize and they cannot readily apply it in practice.

Dr. Sandels believes that young children cannot adapt to the environment of traffic because they are not biologically ready to manage its many demands. She also quotes a Swedish insurance report that the most common error by drivers is lack of caution when passing children, suggesting that drivers know too little about how children can be expected to behave.

Whether or not the Swedish findings directly apply to our country, it is clear that we need to make road safety education more effective and better geared to protect children. Adults may believe that children ought to understand traffic signs and terminology at a particular age; the fact is that many children do not.

Some recommendations for drivers, based on the Swedish Traffic Study:

- *Never expect that a child in traffic, either as a pedestrian or on a bicycle, will behave the same as an adult.*
- *Expect children playing on a sidewalk or at the roadside to be so involved in their game that they may suddenly dash into the street.*
- *Never be sure that children grasp a traffic situation as a whole. Often, they do not. They may notice either only one detail or just a bunch of cars going back and forth.*
- *Children as pedestrians may consider crosswalks as totally safe, especially if there are traffic signals.*
- *Children do not have the same ability as adults to estimate the speed of oncoming cars or their own*

> *speed as they cross the road. This is one reason for*
> *their unexpected "dash-outs."*

- *Never believe that a child has eye contact with you*
  *just because he is looking your way. You can see the*
  *child's eyes, but the child cannot see your expres-*
  *sion until you are quite close since the child is out-*
  *side in bright daylight, while you are sitting in a*
  *dark car.*

Part of the problem with children and traffic is that it is
hard to "prove" where the responsibility lies legally in
small daily events, let alone after a tragedy. A sad story in
the *New York Times* illustrates:

> *Vigils for New York's traffic casualties are coming with*
> *more frequency now. Yesterday, about 35 people, most of*
> *them mothers of school-age children, stood in the rain at*
> *86th Street and Second Avenue. A 10-year-old boy was*
> *killed there last week by a truck that some say barreled*
> *through a red light. The police are not pressing charges; the*
> *boy might have run out in front of it.*

"Some say" the truck barreled through a red light or the
boy "might have" run out in front of it. No one will ever be
sure. This is the reality that parents must face in dealing with
traffic. The message is that children have to be taught to care
for themselves on city streets and highways. Unless they understand what it means to care for themselves fully, adults or
older siblings should remain in charge to protect them.

American parents must take a new traffic problem into
account—the red-light runner who is becoming more and
more of a hazard for adult pedestrians as well as children.
The power of stoplights to control traffic appears to be
waning. The National Safety Council says that ignoring stop

signs, signal lights and laws on yielding right-of-way causes more than one-fourth of all traffic accidents each year.

The flouting of stop signals has become so prevalent that Boston residents tell a story about a cab driver who insists that red lights are just for decoration. In Los Angeles, red-light running has become one of the city's most common traffic violations. And in New York City, former Police Commissioner Robert J. McGuire admitted, "Today it's a 50–50 toss-up whether people will stop for a red light."

Disregard of traffic rules is a relatively new phenomenon. Law-abiding drivers report being harassed by others when they slow down for yellow lights as they approach intersections. Red-light running greatly complicates instructing children about crossing streets and obeying the rules.

"How can you teach a child that when the sign says 'walk', you really can't walk because so many drivers will ignore the red light and drive right on?" asked Roberta de Plas, a New York City mother of two. "I walk my children to school and so do most mothers."

Mrs. de Plas's traffic solution is followed by increasing numbers of parents who are able to be with their children. Others, acknowledging this new problem, give their children more careful instructions (and find themselves becoming more cautious). Still others decide to wait until children are "just a little older" before letting them cross alone.

### Safety Rules for Children as Pedestrians*

1. Cross only at street corners, with the green light and the walk sign.
2. Walk, do not run across the street.
3. Do not trust traffic lights alone, look to make sure the street is clear.

4. Be alert for cars turning, backing up or going through the light.
5. Watch out for bicycles. Many riders ignore traffic rules and go against the flow of traffic.
6. Do not cross between parked cars.
7. Do not fool around while crossing the street. Pushing another child off the curb is not fun. It is not smart to test your will or strength against the drivers of cars.
8. Be extra careful when you cannot see well—in rain, snow, fog or at nightfall. It is more difficult for drivers to see children at these times.

*Adapted from The Parents League of New York

What can you do? The worst course is to pretend that all drivers will be law-abiding. In your street-crossing lessons, you must make it clear that too many people who drive cars do not stop for red lights or stop signs. While you should not excuse such law-breaking, you must tell your child that, until these people are kept off the road, he or she cannot rely on lights alone.

The problem is not helped by the fact that different states have different rules, the most troublesome being that a right turn on a red light is legal in many states, which has encouraged drivers, according to many observers, to ignore red lights altogether. Children must be made aware of this. You might want to join safety groups in their efforts to press for strict enforcement of traffic rules and for uniform regulations throughout the country.

Some suggestions from the Parents League in New York on what you can tell your child: "Do not assume that a driver sees you, or even if he does, that he will stop. Drivers often make legal turns on a green light, but expect pedestrians to get out of the way. Drivers are often in a hurry and think only of getting where they want to go."

It is not easy to tell children about the unfairness of having to watch out more carefully because some people flout the law. It is difficult enough to bring them up to be law-abiding citizens without the example of flagrant but widely tolerated scofflaws all around. More is involved than traffic safety, though that is a primary concern. Teach by example. Tell children that you obey the rules, even though there are others who do not. Two wrongs do not make a right. Perhaps you want to show your child a letter you have written to your representative or the police commissioner asking for better law enforcement.

You can do something constructive by working with a community group in your area. In New York City, for example, a group of concerned parents founded a group called STOP (Stop Traffic Offenses Program) to pressure city officials for more traffic patrols and to urge stiffer penalties for red-light running. Mrs. de Plas, one of the group's organizers, described their successful efforts to increase both citizen and police awareness of the problem. There have been special advertising campaigns and STOP itself, working with the schools, ran a special traffic poster contest to make children more aware of the dangers they face from drivers on city streets. "We had to start somewhere," Mrs. de Plas said, "and running red lights seemed like the best place. No one can say no to us."

## Safety in Cars

More children die from injuries incurred in or around automobiles than from any disease. About one-fourth of the children brought to a hospital emergency room with car-related injuries have been hurt in a "non-crash event," a recent study showed. Some had been injured during a sudden

stop; others were thrown from the car—sometimes they had
opened the door by themselves.

The automobile is the number one killer of children between the ages of one and five, claiming 600 lives each
year, and injuring 40,000 more. Even in minor accidents,
such as fender benders, children can be killed because they
become projectiles, says Patricia Goldman, vice-chairman
of the National Transportation Safety Board. They are
propelled forward. A 30-pound child in a 30 mile-per-hour
crash is ''going to hit the first object it hits with the same impact as if you dropped it out of a third-story window. If you
have a child nestled in your arms and there is an accident
you're not prepared for, you cannot hold on. Your arms are
going to flail open from the impact, thus ejecting the child
from your grasp. The child then becomes a missile, or gets
crushed between the adult and the dashboard.''

However, there is some good news. It is estimated that 90
percent of automobile-related child deaths, and 80 percent
of injuries to children under the age of five, can be prevented by the proper use of restraining devices. An increasing number of states are passing laws requiring that children
ride in special car seats or wear seat belts. And according to
early information from leaders of this new movement, these
laws are saving lives.

Child passenger restraint laws have been passed in the
majority of states and the District of Columbia. In general,
these laws require that children under the age of four or five
ride in a federally approved infant car seat equipped with
special seat belts and protective panels to shield them from
blows to the car and prevent them from being hurled about
in an accident.

Penalties for violations, however, remain low and are
often waived with the purchase of an approved seat. In some
places the state police carry infant car seats to lend to drivers
until they buy their own.

The usage rates for these seats have "tripled and quadrupled since 1978," says Dr. Robert Sanders, the public health director of Rutherford County, Tennessee, credited with heading the movement that in 1970 made that state the first one in the country to enact a child-restraint law.

"We have analyzed case by case every accident since 1979 in which there was a child death," Dr. Sanders says. "In almost every case the child would have survived if he or she had been in an approved seat. Most of them would be alive today, without any doubt."

The safest car seat for infants keeps the baby in a half-reclining position facing the back of the car. Above all, remember that in a car an adult's lap is not a safe place.

For children who weigh under 40 pounds (while children's weights vary, this is usually before the age of four and a half), there are many types of special devices. Most costs range from $30 to $75. Some need installation. It is important to follow the manufacturer's directions in attaching the device to the car and in buckling all the straps. The child should not be able to get free without adult help.

When children reach a weight of 40 to 50 pounds, they can use the standard seat belt. Be sure the lap belt does not go across the child's stomach where it could cause serious injury in an accident. It is sometimes a good idea for a child to sit on a firm cushion two or three inches thick to make sure that the lap belt rides in the proper place, low across the hips. Also, be careful that the shoulder strap does not ride across the child's neck or face.

Mandatory child-restraint laws have found support in many places from police organizations. In Michigan, for example, Sgt. Robert Kraft of the state police praised the law which has been enacted in his state. "It's very frustrating to be driving down the road in a police car and you see this two-year-old standing on the front seat of a moving car, and you've just left an accident a mile up the road where a kid went through the windshield. With this law, we finally have a tool. We can do something about it.''

There has been some resistance to the laws by legislators who cite, among other factors, the expense to poor families. But civic groups often donate devices or sell them at cost. Some employers buy them for the children of employees. In Michigan, the League General Insurance Company of Southfield provided more than 7,000 safety seats free of charge a few years ago to policyholders with small children.

A recent Michigan study, funded by the National Highway Transportation and Safety Board, found that there were half as many injuries to children under the age of four, and one-fourth as many serious injuries and deaths when car seats given by League General were used, compared with injury and fatality rates in a sample of families who had not used the seats.

The laws make sense to many parents already using safety devices, and they may help others to begin. If seat belts are used properly, they greatly reduce the likelihood of injury. The problem is compounded by variations in child-restraint laws from state to state. What is ultimately needed is a model law based on the experiences of several states and adopted throughout the country.

Until then, parents can press for the passage of laws in their individual states and support enforcement of the kind of rules that have been shown effective in reducing traffic fatalities and injuries to children. Education and enforcement efforts by community groups and by state agencies should be supported by everyone interested in safety.

And, last but far from least, parents need to use their own seat belts—every time they are in a car—both for their own safety and to set a good example to their children. As an injury-prevention specialist put it, ''The provision helps children acquire an early habit of seat belt use so that it can be carried over into the really dangerous years for auto accidents when they are 16, 17, and 18.''

# ■ 11 ■

# Risks at Home

## Answering the Door

*I have a four-year-old at home. One of the biggest problems we have with him is when the doorbell is pressed, he goes like a bullet to the front porch and opens the door. He just loves to open the door.*

*It is a slow process, telling him that Mommy or Daddy should be there or someone he knows. You can't open the door for everybody. He's four years old and he is doing fine, but teaching him about that door is hard.*

*Last night, for instance, he heard me on the step and boom the door was opened. The whole family could be in danger from something like this. A child does not have to be alone to create a dangerous situation.*

This is not an average parent talking; it is Detective Jack Meeks of the New York City Police Department. He is also a concerned father who recognizes how important and how difficult it can be to teach a child home safety rules. The policeman's son is a classic illustration of children's wonderful openness and excitement, symbolized here by wanting to open the door to welcome everyone.

It is too bad that we cannot open our doors to the world the way a four-year-old would like to. Unfortunately, we must teach our children to discriminate between those they can trust and unknown strangers. And just as you have to teach children safety measures outside the home, you also need to teach the techniques for reducing the possibility of harm or trouble coming to them at home.

When and how to answer the door is a good place to begin. It is, of course, best if young children are not left alone, but it is unrealistic not to prepare them for the eventuality that they may have to answer the doorbell whether or not there are adults around.

Preschoolers, who find it hard to make distinctions, should be told simply not to open the door at all. That is the safest tactic. Your instructions to them might include telling them to say something like "My mom doesn't allow me to open the door. She is busy. Who wants to come in?"

Children who feel uncomfortable for *any* reason, no matter at what age, should be told not to open the door. And, of course, starting with them as young as you can, you teach children not to let any strangers in the house, no matter what they say.

A good example to use when you are playing your "What if?" games is to tell a child what to do when a stranger asks for help in a particular situation. Given the opportunity, most children find it difficult to resist being helpful. Ask "What would you do if a woman rang the doorbell and asked to come in and use the phone because her car had broken down and she needed help?" This would disarm most children, and they would want to let the woman in. The correct answer is not to open the door. To be helpful, the child could offer to make the call for her while she waits outside.

Some other hypothetical situations to try: What if the visitor claimed to be a repairman? (You have told your children you will let them know in advance if you are expecting anyone to work in the house and not to let anyone in unless specifically expected.)

What if the visitor had a package he said he wanted to deliver? (He can leave it outside the front door or come back later when Mommy or Daddy is available. Tell children specifically not to pick up the package.)

What if the visitor claims to have a message from either Mommy or Daddy? (If the visitor is a neighbor known to the child who is uncertain about opening the door or the child does not want to, the message can be slipped through the door.) If it is a stranger, it should be a long-established family policy that you will never send messages through an unknown person. (Some families find that having a special password works well for them in this kind of situation. But it is not necessary to be that elaborate, risking all sorts of confusion.)

As they grow older and ready for greater responsibility, children need to learn how to lock and unlock the doors to the house. If you are wondering at what age a child can answer the door alone, be guided by when he or she learns to lock and unlock doors and the interest displayed in doing this. You should install a peephole and children should be taught to use it, even if they have to stand on a chair to see through it.

Here again, responses appropriate for the particular home situation should be practiced. When the doorbell rings, asking "Who is it?" is not enough. Children must learn how to decide whether or not to open the door. A good principle for guidance is when in doubt, don't open the door. In this area, caution is better than taking risks.

Children also need to be taught that doors must always be locked, even when they are at home. It should become second nature to them to lock the door *after* they come home. Unless it is a habit, it is easy for both children and adults to forget. Burglaries do occur in the daytime as well as at night. Locking the door when you are at home is an important precaution.

A word about keys. In general, police and safety experts suggest that you plan ahead whenever possible so that you will not be tempted to hide a key under the doormat or to tell your children to pick one up there. Detective Thomas Oates of the Montclair (New Jersey) Police Department says that it is never a good idea to hide keys anywhere outside of your own house. "Burglars know the best places. If you must hide a key, hide it at a neighbor's house, never at your own."

## Leaving Children Home Alone

At what age you leave a child at home alone without adult supervision is just as much an individual matter as when you permit them to cross streets alone or grant other privileges. Ideally, you start leaving a child alone for short daytime periods when you go out on errands. See if both you and the child are comfortable with the arrangement. Then, as a child gets older, you can extend the time and the occasions. Leaving children at night without a baby-sitter is another big step. Sometimes parents forget that even if children seem mature and appear able to handle being alone, they may still at times be frightened or merely lonesome for some company.

Many children are worried about being left at home alone and may feel like 12-year-old Maura Coniff of South Plainfield, New Jersey, one of many children who wrote to

President Reagan and the House Select Committee on Children, Youth and Families. "It seems there is no place save anymore, not even the home, where most murders and robberies are committed. We are afraid to be alone at home because of this constant fear."

The Children's Defense Fund, a child advocacy group, estimates that there are between six and seven million "latchkey" children in the United States. The term refers to children between the ages of three and fifteen who may wear their house keys around their necks and are left alone regularly during some period of the day. Some are responsible for the care of younger brothers and sisters.

There is no magic age at which children are suddenly ready to be left alone. Most parents agree that sometime between the ages of seven and ten, children are responsible enough to spend some time at home by themselves. In some cases circumstances make it necessary to leave children alone earlier than we would like. Whether your children are alone every day after school while you are at work or only occasionally while you run errands, you can make the unsupervised time safer and more fun for them:

*1. Have at least one home fire drill.* Be sure children know where the exits they must use are located. If you live in an apartment building, caution them against using the elevator in case of fire. Be sure they know the location of fire stairs or escapes.

Detective Thomas Oates reports that most children who have participated in a Montclair safety education program "Be Prepared," were not aware of what to do in case of a fire in their homes. "We tell them not to try to put the fire out themselves. They should be sure they get out of the house quickly, then attempt to notify the fire department. We also tell them that they and their families should have a fire escape-plan mapped out and kept in readiness." Under such a plan, all family members know a central place to meet, such as a nearby tree or light pole so that everyone can be accounted for.

Tips for fire prevention safety also come from the Sesame Street Fire Safety Project of the Children's Television Workshop. (a) Point out the best emergency exits to use in each room. (b) Teach older children to feel an exit door before opening it. If the door is hot or smoke is coming from under it, use an alternative route. (c) Remind family members that doors should be closed after leaving a room to prevent fire from spreading. (d) Practice the "stop, drop and roll" method to be used if clothing catches fire. (Stop immediately where you are, Drop to the floor and Roll over and over until the fire is out.)

The Children's Television Workshop urges special consideration be given in teaching preschool children how to cope with fire emergencies. They may not understand all your directions. Very young children cannot be expected to leave a building alone or decide which route to take in an emergency. They must be guided. Also, a firefighter in full gear, including air mask and ax, can look frightening to young children. Sometimes they hide from firefighters who come to rescue them. Try to give your young child some positive ideas about firefighters using pictures or, if you have the time, a visit to the firehouse.

2. *Instruct children in how to behave if they suspect a burglary.* If children arrive home from school and find everything in suspicious disarray, they should not, as some children might try to do, attempt to look around the house for an intruder. "They could find themselves in a face-to-face confrontation with an intruder who is still hiding in the home," says Oates.

The safest thing for a child to do, he says, is to either go back to school and ask someone there to call the police or go to a neighbor's house to call the police. In general, children are reluctant to call the police, Oates reports, because they are afraid of feeling foolish should they be mistaken in their suspicions. "We tell them we'd rather come out for 100 false alarms than miss one crime," Oates says, adding that more crimes are solved by people calling directly than through expensive long-term investigations after the fact.

*3. Review phone procedures.* Be sure your children know whom to call in an emergency and whom they can call if they are merely lonesome.

*4. Review door answering procedures.* Do not let strangers into the house.

*5. Review basic home safety rules.* Do not use the stove or oven or microwave or climb on furniture or ladders. Don't play with matches or use knives or other sharp objects without an adult present.

*6. Have children call you routinely at work as soon as they get home from school.* You'll know they are all right and, if possible, you can talk a little about their day at school. Let them know there are times you may be unavoidably late in getting home because of a work deadline or a flat tire or some other mishap. If they are uncomfortable for any reason, this is the time for them to call a relative, friend or neighbor.

*7. Train children to keep keys out of sight on the street.* A child with a highly visible set of keys coming home from school is easily recognized as being alone and unsupervised. Each child should have his or her own set on a good-looking, sturdy key chain, which is different from everyone else's in the family. Never write any names and addresses on keys. If lost, you can replace them without the likelihood that a potential burglar can use them. If you are in doubt when keys are lost, have your lock changed.

8. *Arrange to have snacks on hand within children's easy reach.* Snacks that require no cooking—peanut butter, crackers, cold cereal, cheese, fruit or raw vegetables are best. (What you do about junk foods depends on how you deal with them the rest of the time.) Keep plastic cups, juice and milk containers readily available.

9. *Make a simple and easy-to-find first-aid kit.* Label and instruct the child in its use.

10. *Work out in advance policies about how much television to watch and when to do their homework.*

One question you must settle is whether or when children may have friends come and visit. It may be easier to restrict the home just for the family, particularly if your older child is responsible for watching a younger sibling. Under such circumstances, the best rule is no visiting friends. Your children have each other for company.

If, however, a child is alone, a friend may provide valuable companionship. You may be able to work out an arrangement with another parent of an only child in the class, with alternating weeks at each other's homes.

We found with our children that some of their friends were more responsible than others, and that had to be talked about frankly. Some friends were fine to have over alone, while others we did not trust to the same extent because they were less mature. Just as our boys preferred some of our friends, we liked some of their friends better than others. If you are going to have a variable set of operating rules, it is important to establish that you will have the final say. Children recognize that some of their peers could make life more difficult if there were no adults around.

It is, of course, easier to make a simple rule: no visiting friends while no adults are at home. A policeman I talked to established this rule for his older children when they were baby-sitting for their younger siblings. This leaves no question about who is responsible if there is trouble. You may find this a comfortable and safe family rule. Trying to distinguish between different friends and situations may require more discussion and energy for decision-making than you can afford. The important thing is to think over in advance how you want to handle this situation and then follow through.

In different parts of the country, there are community organizations interested in helping children who have to be home alone. One is called PhoneFriend, an after-school telephone help line operated by a branch of the American Association of University Women in State College, Pennsylvania. It serves about 4,500 elementary school children. The average age of the callers is eight years old.

"We call ourselves a help line or a warm line rather than a hot line," says Marilyn Keat, one of the project organizers. "We do provide help if children call with crisis-type calls, but we don't want the children to feel that they have to have a serious problem. Children can call if they feel lonely or scared or if they think they've heard a noise. One child called because he thought there was a snake in the living room."

There are now several children's telephone assistance lines operating. For example, in the Chicago area, there is Kidsline, which serves a reported 60,000 children younger than 13 on a 24-hour basis.

Some observers, however, are concerned that Phone-Friend and other hot lines may become a substitute for adult supervision for children under 10. "PhoneFriend can be great," says Lynette Long, an assistant professor of education at Loyola College in Baltimore, who along with her husband, Thomas, has written a handbook for latchkey children and their parents. "But it does not fill the void of not having an adult in the neighborhood you can depend on."

In their research, the Longs found that children were telling them they were afraid, lonely and bored. These feelings are often not told to parents, the researchers claim, because children are sensitive to increasing stress in their parents. In addition, these children get positive feedback for acting like "big" boys and girls.

"Ideally," Dr. Long continues, "more day-care and community centers with services for latchkey children are the answer, and schools will increasingly have to see themselves as child-care providers."

These phone lines can be valuable additions to a system of services available to school children. But others also caution there is a danger that some parents might think phone conversations are taking the place of daily personal contact and supervision by a competent adult. Nina White, Phone-Friend's director of operations, says, "We don't feel that this is the only answer, but it is a way that communities can be supportive."

Evie Herrmann-Keeling, executive director of Parents Anonymous in Hartford, Connecticut, who has offered a five-part series of weekly courses for latchkey children and their parents at a local corporation, agrees. She does not want families to regard the existence of her program as "permission to leave kids alone after school. Even though for many families," she adds, "financial necessity leaves them little choice.

"In most companies after 3 P.M., there is a lot of quiet telephoning. Parents feel they have to check and see if their children arrived home safe. But it is really foolish for this sort of thing to have to be underground. If companies can become more supportive of families, workers would be more productive.''

The course is limited to children nine and older of the Phoenix Mutual Life Insurance Company employees. Mrs. Herrmann-Keeling believes that it is ''not appropriate for children under nine to be in self-care.'' She prefers the phrase ''self-care'' to the term ''latchkey'' child, because the latter has become somewhat pejorative.

She discovered the program at a conference and thought it would be right for Hartford. The course materials were developed by the ''I'm in Charge'' Project of the Kansas Committee for the Prevention of Child Abuse.

The first session is for parents alone. ''Often parents do not realize that their kids can be scared and lonely when they are alone.'' The following three sessions are for the children only, concentrating on home safety skills, emergency responses and care of younger siblings. The final meeting brings parents and children together to discuss issues raised during earlier classes.

''We want families to develop children's sense of responsibility and involve parents in monitoring their progress. We want parents and children to understand that they are working together to achieve a common goal,'' says Mrs. Herrmann-Keeling.

Generally, it is not a good idea to assume that children know all the home safety procedures with the degree of detail and sophistication that you hope for. It is important to review these matters specifically and not to take things for granted. Some parents say, ''Jane is only nine—'' but nevertheless treat her as if she were 14. That is unfair to your child.

Also, many parents, especially when things are going well, forget to praise their children for acting responsibly and grown up or to say they are proud of them. Most children will rise to difficult occasions. Your trust helps them develop a sense of responsibility and self-confidence.

## Answering the Phone

Every parent knows how fascinating the telephone is to young children and how they race to answer it soon after they have learned to talk. I remember when our older son was two. He picked up the phone and in answer to the obvious question, "Is your mother home?" replied "Yes, she is" and hung up. We never found out who it was. But Paul eventually learned that the question meant the caller wanted to talk to Mommy, not just find out if she was home.

Young children usually love to talk over the phone and will often have longer conversations with adults than they ever would person to person. They like to show off how much they know, and since they tend to be trusting, it is important to teach them as early as possible the safe way to answer the phone and what they should say in different situations.

Not very long ago, children used to be told to answer the phone by saying something like, "This is the Jones residence, Elizabeth speaking" or some similar phrases of identification. Safety experts now advise not to do this. The phone should be answered only by saying, "Hello," and then waiting for callers to identify themselves. And it is the caller's responsibility to state the reason for the call. If you follow this procedure, your child will be more likely to as well.

Asked why you don't say more until you know who is on the line, you can explain simply that it is safer this way. "There are some crazy people around, and we don't want them bothering us." Once children are old enough, you can tell them that some people call to find out your name and address and at what times you are likely to be out so they can break in. "So we don't give out any information to callers we do not know."

It is very difficult for children (and even for some adults) not to answer questions or even give their names when people ask politely. We tend to be afraid of hurting someone's feelings. Children need to learn that they can, and should, refuse to give out any personal information on the phone and that the callers should identify themselves first. This is another instance where they have to unlearn uniform "nice" behavior in the interest of safety. Be sure to tell them that if a stranger says something that scares or bothers them or if they do not understand, they are to hang up the phone.

"What should I say when someone on the phone asks me 'Who is this?' or 'Whose residence is this?' " your child may ask. Tell him or her to reply, "Who is calling, please?" If the caller is persistent, the child can say "My parents told me not to tell anyone my name until I know who is calling," or he or she should simply hang up. It is amazing how rarely this option occurs to children, partly because they have been taught to defer to adults and also because they are not yet used to getting their own calls and like to talk on the phone.

Warn children not to volunteer information about the schedules and whereabouts of family members. Even if no safety rules were involved, it is none of the caller's business unless they are relatives or close friends.

It is especially important for children never to tell strangers that they are alone at home. Even if you only leave a child alone once in a while and only for short periods, he or she should know how to answer the phone in the safest possible manner.

If a child answers the phone before you get home, he or she should say, "I'm sorry, Mommy can't come to the phone right now." And add, "She is sleeping" or "She is in the shower. Please leave your name and number and I'll ask her

to call you back.'' You should have a pad and pencil next to
the phone. Even before a child is ready to be left alone, you
will want to go over the best phone responses to give.

## Important Phone Numbers

Every family with children should have their important phone numbers posted near the phone:

> Mother's Office
> Father's Office
> Neighbor or relative at home
> Pediatrician
> Police Department
> Fire Department
> Local emergency ambulance

A family living in an apartment building may want
to list the number of the building superintendent. In a
single-parent household, if possible, the home and office phone numbers of the nonresident parent should
also be listed.

There are some ''pretend'' phone conversations you can
rehearse with your children. If they want to practice speaking into the phone, let them do it. You will be telling them
repeatedly not to give out personal information, but always
emphasize what you want them to say instead. Some ideas:

- *"Hi. Your mother ordered a magazine subscription
  and I'm checking to see if the name and address
  I have is correct."*
- *"This is Smith's Department Store. We are deliv-
  ering your package tomorrow at 2 o'clock. Will
  anyone be home?"*
- *"I'm Joe Jones, a friend of your father's. We grew*

*up together in Ohio. I'm in town for a few days. I want to come and see him. Will the family be home this weekend?''*

In each case, the idea you are getting across is not to answer the questions—a hard concept for children to learn. Reassure them that if these callers are on the level, they will phone again later and will respect them for handling the phone in a grown-up manner. Children need not worry that people will not like them. They can also say ''I don't know'' to any of the questions. But it is hard for children who have just learned their address and phone number to say they don't know them.

While you discuss the phone, your children may enjoy the story of the eccentric old man who never answered his telephone. When his neighbor asked him why, he said, ''I had the phone put in for my convenience, not for other people's.''

In addition, you will want to show children how the phone can help them in emergencies. Here also they need to practice what to do if the need should arise. Again, pretend conversations to rehearse for various contingencies are a good idea. Try to get a little fun into some sessions. You can pretend to make a call, not giving enough information: ''Susie just fainted. Send help.'' Ask your children to tell you what is ''wrong'' with your performance and how they would correct it.

With young children, you may want to instruct them in how to dial. For an emergency, they can quickly be taught to dial ''0'' for the operator or 911 if your area uses that number. You can check with your local authorities to see what procedures are preferred.

## Baby-sitting Safety Tips

Parents sometimes fail to realize that they need to make baby-sitters and others who take care of their children aware of home safety procedures. Most parents only ask the persons they know are responsible to baby-sit. They check out references of their reliability. (Teenagers who are sitting for a family for the first time are also well advised to make sure they know who referred them to a particular family before they accept the job.)

The first time someone cares for your children, you should allow for some extra time to acquaint him or her with the house as well as the children. In particular, you want to make sure that the person knows where the phone extensions are, how to lock the front door and how to reach you or another family member in an emergency. If you live in an apartment, go over the workings of the housephone as well.

A quick tour of the house is in order. Point out where you keep the emergency phone numbers posted. Explain how any special lights or equipment works and show sitters how you operate your stove, your television, stereo and anything else they may be using. You will probably want to show the location of the fuse box as well. Have a note pad handy so it will be easy for your sitter to take phone messages.

After explaining the door locks, tell the sitter where you keep a spare key, just in case someone gets locked out of the house. Explain your smoke detector system and any burglar alarms you may have installed. Point out the medicine cabinet with first-aid supplies.

None of this need take much time, but you want the sitter to feel comfortable and competent. You can say, as we usually did, knowing about all these things is like carrying an umbrella on a cloudy day. If you are prepared, the chances are that you will not need to use your knowledge.

Don't overwhelm a first-time sitter, but convey the fact

that certain rules are important for his or her safety as well as for your children's. You may want to begin by saying, ''I'm sure you already know most of these things, but I think it is a good idea that we go over some of them together:''

- *Do not open the door to strangers and don't let anyone who comes know that you are alone. (Tell them explicitly you will not be upset if they do not open the door for relatives and friends they do not know and are not expected. If you are expecting someone to stop by, tell your sitter in advance and give some description; otherwise they should not let anyone in.)*
- *Take phone messages for us, if possible without letting callers know you are home alone. Do not give out our name and phone number; let callers identify themselves.*
- *If you smell smoke or see fire in the house, quickly get the children and yourself out; then call the fire department.*
- *It is a good idea to say directly that you would rather they take precautions that might turn out not to have been necessary than to risk the children's safety and their own. Tell them this is your safety philosophy.*

Go over your house rules. Most people do not allow visits by the sitter's friends, except for special occasions agreed on in advance. You want to make sure that a sitter does not talk on the phone all night, tying up the line. A ban on smoking and drinking alcoholic beverages is a good idea. On the other hand, do invite sitters to raid your refrigerator for snacks and soft drinks.

No matter how many times someone sits for you, you will always want to leave a number where you can be reached. We always put up the number alongside all the emergency phone numbers in a central location.

Responsibility is a two-way street between you and your babysitter. You should let a sitter know approximately when you expect to return and try to be reasonably on time, unless you can call to say that you will be late. You want to assure sitters that their personal safety is important to you. A good way to do this is to be considerate, go over your requirements in advance and make it clear that you will make the necessary arrangements for your sitter's safe return to his or her home, if you are not taking the sitter home yourself. If your sitters know you care about their safety, they will quite naturally be more intent on assuring your child's safety as well.

# ◼ 12 ◼

# If Your Child Is Missing

ONE of the most frightening experiences a parent can have is to discover that a child is missing. Fears of abduction and kidnapping come almost immediately to mind. Children, especially preschoolers, often do wander off. But in most instances, the scene ends happily like the one reported by the mother of a three-year-old who, together with a friend, simply walked out the front door of their house toward a busy commercial street. After a few minutes, worried because the children seemed to be playing unusually quietly, the mother decided to check and found them gone. Both members searched frantically in the house and surrounding area. After 40 minutes of agonized frenzy—with the neighborhood mobilized for a search and the police having established a command center—the two children were discovered in a pizza parlor trying to order on credit.

Although many children are free-spirited with some of Huck Finn in them, preschoolers are particularly vulnerable when they strike out on adventures by themselves. And the best antidote is prevention.

Younger children should be watched closely at all times. ''With my child, who is four years old,'' says police Detective Jack Meeks, ''we let him go out alone only when someone in the family can keep an eye on him. You can tell him 'Don't go past here or only go to there.' But periodically you have to look out and see where he is. You know he is a child. You just can't walk away from him and say 'I want to go shopping, I'll be back in an hour.' You can tell them at this age to stay put and they might—and then again they might not. With my four-year-old, we watch. If a kid is gone, he is gone.'' Lieutenant Michael Fitzgerald of the District of Columbia Special Investigation Branch adds that ''any child under six is automatically listed as a critical situation by Missing Persons.''

An effective preventive measure is for parents to walk through the neighborhood with their children and explain just where the safe parameters are. These will change and vary with the age of the child. If possible, inform neighbors what the child's boundaries are. Keep all explanation simple and, if in doubt whether to leave a child alone in a particular place—Don't.

The biggest mistake that parents can make if they think a child is missing is not calling the police soon enough. A police expert says, ''If you lose a small child at 3:15, start worrying at 3:20 and call the police by 3:30. Know where the kid is supposed to be and if he's not there, call the police. The sooner a search is organized, the easier it will be to find a child.'' Lieutenant Fitzgerald adds, ''Some people feel that they shouldn't call the police for either eight or 24 hours. They may believe in a fictitious rule that people aren't considered missing by the police for 24 hours." *Another officer says simply that parents should wait no longer to report a missing child than it takes to perceive that the child is lost.

### Practical Steps to Reduce the Chances Your Child Will Be Lost or Abducted

1. Know where your child is at all times.
2. Do not leave your child alone in your car or yard, in a store or any other place.
3. Do not put your child's name on his or her clothing or books. The name on the tag can put a potential abductor on a first-name basis with your child.
4. Make sure that your children know how to use the telephone and know your telephone number (including area code) and that they also know to call the police in an emergency.
5. Walk your child around your immediate neighborhood and explain which places are off limits.
6. Teach your child what to do if he or she is lost.
7. Even when your children reach an age when they can play without constant adult supervision, you should still know where they are. This might be a good time to investigate joining or starting a "neighborhood watch" program. It should include establishing a 'safe house' on each block that children are taught to recognize, run by a qualified adult. This is a good idea for children's general personal safety and can also serve as a refuge from gangs or bullies as well as a place to get help if there is an accident.

As soon as you notify the authorities, enlist your neigh-

---

*The confusion occurs because the FBI has a requirement that it will not become involved in a case unless 24 hours have passed. It is then presumed that the child could have been taken out of state and it is a federal matter. The FBI would also become involved if there is a ransom note.

bors and older children to help. They know your child and can recognize him or her from a distance and they may have additional ideas about places children are likely to go. The police will have only your description and perhaps a photograph or fingerprints. Gloria Yerkovich of Child Find, Inc., a child tracking agency with contacts across the country, says that people generally do not know that the fire department, in addition to the police department, can be enlisted to join the search team.

Investigations of a report of a missing child vary little from place to place. For small children, a search of the area where they were last seen begins and almost always, according to the police, turns up the child.

If the child is not found immediately, family, friends and area residents are interviewed. A house-to-house search may be made. The police try to determine whether the child has left home deliberately, although children of a certain age, usually younger than ten, are assumed not to have done so. Teletype descriptions are sent to police departments in other parts of the country, if necessary.

Should your child be found, notify the police. Never assume they will be told by someone else. And if a small child comes to your house unexpectedly and without any explanation, contact the parents or the police. Do not assume that the family knows where a child has wandered.

"We get kids who are separated from their classes or kids who can't find their parents," says Charles Bonaventura, a New York police officer. "And they get hysterical. First thing you know, you have this little tyke surrounded by mountains of people. Then somebody calls the police.

"We respond. We try to calm him down. We take him to the station house. We give him candy. We pick up the child and let him hold a police hat or whistle or play with a nightstick. We try to find out about him, if possible.

"Usually a mother or teacher will call us and say, 'I'm missing a child.' But there is frequently a time lapse before we get enough information. If we had the information at the beginning, all the child's misery would never be. We would bring the child right to the school or home.

"That's why we believe that even young kids should know their full names, how to spell them, where they live and their phone number. On trips they should have some sort of identification paper with them.

"What I do with my son, who is six, is to make sure that if he becomes lost he knows his address and phone number. I have him repeat them a few times so I am sure he knows. If he was upset, he might be confused. But I know if a police officer was able to calm him down he would be able to tell where he lived."

As children get older (between the ages of five and eight), they need very specific instructions from parents about what to do in various situations should they get lost. It is vital to teach children their addresses and telephone numbers at the youngest possible age. In addition, they should be taught how to handle themselves with strangers (see Chapter 8), and how to seek help from the nearest person in authority. Then they will know where to turn in an emergency.

With a little advance planning and some family instructions, there are ways to minimize the chances that your child will get lost or abducted. When going into a crowded place, plan where you will meet if anyone, not just children, becomes separated from the family or group. Who will accompany whom to the rest room should be established before you leave home, stressing the fact that you do not want children going alone. If you will be near water, safety rules should be set down firmly. No one, adults as well as children, should ever go swimming alone.

## If Your Child Is Missing
### (After You Have Notified the Police)

1. Someone who knows the child should stay at home in case he or she returns. Otherwise, finding the house empty, a child may wander off again.
2. Keep your telephone attended at all times.
3. Be sure to check every room in your house—under beds, behind the furniture—the child may have fallen asleep.
4. Check every house and building in the neighborhood. Look into empty cartons, abandoned refrigerators, washers and dryers.
5. File information about your missing child with the Federal Bureau of Investigation so it can be fed into the FBI's National Crime Information Center Computer (NCIC).
6. If you are going to print posters or flyers or give interviews to local radio and television stations or newspapers, do not give your home address and phone number. This will avoid most extortion threats and crank calls. If you receive such calls or threats, report them to the police.

One father, tired of looking for children in shopping malls, has developed a system that may work for other parents. First, he believes that everyone, not just the driver, should take note of where the car is parked. "I tell everybody to remember level three because I might forget," he says. Also, he has noticed that there is usually some kind of arcade or place with video games where children gravitate. This is his choice for a meeting place. It is easy to find and there is no problem with elementary school children not remembering where it is. Younger children, ages three to seven, are the ones whose hands are always held or who are always watched carefully on family outings.

Estimates of the number of children abducted each year vary a great deal and most of the figures given are unreliable, reports Howard Davidson, director of the National Legal Resource Center for Child Advocacy and Protection at the American Bar Association. Estimates on the number of children abducted by strangers range from 25,000 to 50,000; the range of those taken by the noncustodial parent is even wider, from 100,000 to 300,000 each year.* "There is a need for scientific research in this area in terms of statistics," Davidson says.

## Have Information about Your Child
## Ready and On Hand

1. Take a full-face photograph of your child at least every six months. On the back write the child's present height and weight; clothing and shoe size. List any distinguishing features—birthmarks, scars, dimples, etc.
2. Know where your child's dental and medical X-rays and fingerprints are. If you move, be sure to take them with you.
3. Be aware of your child's habits, friends, special abilities and shortcomings. Most parents overlook familiar mannerisms of their children which can be of great importance. List anything about your child that may be unique. A recognizable voice pattern or sound, a stutter, a special laugh, a way of walking or certain expressions that are easily identifiable.
4. Child Find, Inc. recommends that you obtain a Social Security card as well as a certified copy of

*There is one researcher whose estimates are even higher.

your child's birth certificate and an individual passport for each child.
5. Do not wait until you might need it to put together all the information about your child.

Statistics on cases of missing children often include runaways, children kidnapped by divorced or separated parents as well as those abducted by strangers or who wander off by themselves. With all the different figures given, one factor is a constant: namely, the estimates of children taken by a parent in a divorce case are always higher than the estimates of those taken by strangers. Each year, according to experts, 1.8 million children are reported missing. This high figure includes runaways, of whom about 90 percent turn up unharmed within a few days. Others end up as victims of violence.

The fact is that there is no reliable national network for counting the number of children who are abducted, let alone for locating them. "We do a much better job keeping track of automobiles, guns and refrigerators than we do of missing children," says Senator Paula Hawkins of Florida, who, with Representative Paul Simon of Illinois, co-sponsored the Missing Children's Act, signed into law in October 1982.

Under this law, the federal government can be enlisted in the searches for missing children. Parents may place information and descriptions into the FBI National Crime Information Computer. The computer, which contains a national compilation of facts about missing children, alerts police across the country.

The two cases that moved lawmakers to action were the disappearance of six-year-old Etan Patz near a New York City school bus stop and the kidnapping of Adam Walsh, also six years old, from a Hollywood, Florida, shopping center. Etan has never been found. Adam's severed head was all that was found two weeks after his disappearance. His abduction and murder prompted many parents in the Hollywood area to protect their children more carefully than in the past. Mrs. Linda Blank, a neighbor, said neither of her two children is allowed to play alone in the playground of the school across from their home any longer.

Passage of the Missing Children's Act showed that there is at last a national recognition of the serious and all-too-frequent tragedy of missing children, says Howard Davidson. "Public awareness has been awakened. Greater numbers of children are reported missing. The number of records on file has been going up. It is an important beginning." Gloria Yerkovich adds that there are now more law enforcement officers working on the problem. She says the legislation has stimulated local law enforcement agencies to be more sensitive to the issue. But many difficulties still remain.

The growing number of estranged parents who snatch a child to hurt a former spouse presents a complicating factor in dealing with missing children. Kidnapping by parents, also called child abductions, child snatching, legal kidnapping and custody kidnapping, has been given increasing attention by children's advocates, legislators and social scientists in recent years.

A 1982 national study of parental kidnapping found that there are many more such abductions than had earlier been believed. The study estimates that there are at least 313,000 incidents each year and possibly as many as 626,000. The research was conducted by Richard Gelles, a sociology professor at the University of Rhode Island. The results are based on telephone interviews with 3,745 adults.

Of that number 1.5 percent, 55 respondents, reported that they had been involved in an incident of child snatching by parents within the previous 12 months. Based on that finding, Dr. Gelles projected the number of incidents of child snatching which occur each year. He cautioned that the high figure represented a maximum number of possible kidnappings. It includes both long-term and short-term incidents, failure to return a child after a visit as well as actual abductions.

Dr. Gelles nevertheless believes the high figure is significant because it is the first such estimate based on empirical evidence. Other estimates by law enforcement groups and the press have set the figures lower, between 100,000 and 300,000.

The survey was conducted with the help of the polling firm Louis Harris and Associates and was supported by a grant from the National Institute of Justice.

Child snatching is escalating as the number of divorces goes up, says Child Find's Gloria Yerkovich. It has been estimated that one out of every ten divorces involves a child abduction. The 1980 Federal Parent Kidnapping Prevention Act provides government support for a parent whose child has been kidnapped by a separated or divorced spouse. The act requires that all states obey the Uniform Child Custody Jurisdiction Act honoring custody orders from other states and expands the use of federal parent-locator services, which track down parents through tax records and employment papers. It also authorizes the FBI to help local agencies find a child-stealing parent when the state has issued an arrest warrant.

But many observers who have been involved in missing child cases believe that the Parent Kidnapping Act is difficult to enforce because it has enough loopholes to allow an offender to escape by taking a child to another state. In addition, since child stealing frequently occurs before a custody hearing takes place, the act often does not even apply.

Whatever the numbers and the laws, the sad fact is that parents are forcefully abducting their own children. As a consequence, many schools require all parents to complete forms indicating which other adults are authorized to pick up a child. Schools are especially careful in dealing with children of divorced parents, trying to determine whether the non-custodial parent may pick up the child for any reason— even for something as seemingly harmless as a dental appointment. Still, incidents and problems do arise.

John Ourth, principal at Oak Terrace School in Highwood, Illinois, has developed special "Kidnap Alert" procedures for his school. And, in addition, he says, "As a general policy, we permit no student to leave the grounds alone. Any parent who wants to pick up a child during the school day, *no matter what the purpose,* must come to the school office to do so. We require identification from any adult we don't recognize who comes to pick up a child. We reserve the right not to release the child to anyone other than the custodial parent; in cases of coubt, we phone the custodial parent to confirm that someone else has been authorized to pick up a youngster."

Mr. Ourth reports that when he first announced this policy, parents complained that it was too rigid. "But after I explained it and it went into effect, the dominant reaction was 'I like this. I know my child is safe.' "

## Fingerprinting for Small Fingers?

Your kindergarten child may bring home a note suggesting that you have him or her fingerprinted. Don't be surprised or indignant. This does not mean that the school has spotted early criminal tendencies. What it does mean is that your community wants to take a positive step to lower the number of children who are missing every year. Thousands of children in more than a dozen states around the country—New York, Virginia, Florida, Georgia, New Jersey,

California, Pennsylvania, Massachusetts, Nebraska, Connecticut, Rhode Island, Kansas, Illinois and Indiana—are being fingerprinted voluntarily as a means of identifying them should they be reported missing.

Though there have been some objections that taking fingerprints violates a child's rights, many parents prefer to take this precaution. And in most states, the only copy of the prints is turned over to the parents for safekeeping. In some places, however, the police have retained the fingerprints, a procedure vehemently opposed by local branches of the American Civil Liberties Union.

"There is a serious potential for invasions of individual privacy," says William Olds, executive director of the Connecticut branch of the ACLU. "The fingerprints could be misused at some point and involve children in criminal investigations." Mr. Olds said he did not object to police departments fingerprinting children so long as the prints were turned over to the parents.

Among those who have spoken out publicly against fingerprinting is Dr. Benjamin Spock, the noted pediatrician. He opposes the practice, even if voluntary on the part of parents. "Children are not going to say, 'This is against my constitutional rights.' We should be taking better care of children—specifically through day-care centers, after-school programs and social services instead of using police methods to keep track of them." Dr. Spock believes that fingerprinting is a "blind alley" that "gives parents a false sense of security and does nothing to prevent kidnapping."

Others say that fingerprinting children can create an atmosphere of fear. A New Jersey ACLU executive said he was worried that "kids might potentially feel they are doing something wrong and that's why they are having their fingerprints taken."

But many others favor the procedure. Sister Maureen James, principal of St. Elizabeth's School in Union County,

New Jersey, says, "If we save one child, it's worth it." A mother in New Jersey said, "Unless you're planning a life of crime for your child, I can't see why any parent would object." And 13-year-old Michele Mauro commented, "If anything ever happens, they've got a way of finding me." The FBI calls the new fingerprinting programs "invaluable," but urges that parents, not the police, should keep the records. Parents should keep fingerprinting cards with their personal papers.

Among the strongest supporters of fingerprinting programs are the parents of children who have been kidnapped. Stanley Patz, Etan's father, favors the process as a means of preventing children from being enrolled in schools under assumed names. Another staunch advocate is Marjan Martin, whose five-year-old daughter, Maria, was abducted while the family was vacationing in San Diego and was found alive 10 days later. She says, "When my child was missing, the police needed fingerprints, pictures and dental charts, and I didn't have anything to give them."

Twice, she remembers, "they thought they found a little girl who matched my daughter's description and I had to suffer the agony of looking at those children who were strangers. If I had had fingerprints, they could have matched them up and spared me some of the anxiety."

Fingerprinting is helpful, Gloria Yerkovich agrees, even though it is not going to protect your child from being abducted. But it will aid in any search, even if only to eliminate possibilities. It is often important to make negative identifications. The children stolen most frequently are from three to twelve years old, when physical descriptions change rapidly and photos quickly become outdated. They are frequently too young to know their former address or even their last names.

Charles Sutherland, who publishes SEARCH, a quarterly report for law enforcement agencies about missing persons, says, "A law enforcement agency with fingerprints and a picture to work with is miles ahead of where it usually has to start, in trying to find a missing child." He cautions that fingerprints will not find a missing child; they only help in identifications. "What law enforcement officers need the most is an accurate description. They cannot look for a four-year-old child successfully if all they have is a picture of a two-year-old."

In fact, it is a good idea to assemble and keep a full identification portfolio for your child in a readily accessible place. In addition to fingerprints and dental records, you should include a good photograph with the date, a listing of physical characteristics, even a lock of hair. In the case of fingerprints, remember that they are for your own private use only. There should only be one set with you as parents the sole persons who have access to it.

When you are thinking about getting your child's fingerprints, there are some other things to bear in mind. First, avoid any business that charges for the process or wants to sell you a do-it-yourself package. You will find that community programs are almost always free. Also, the prints you get will be more reliable. Second, explain to your child what is being done and why so that there can be no misunderstanding or unnecessary concern.

If your community does not have a fingerprinting program, call the information section of your local police station or sheriff to see about getting one started.

Some help on how to search for a missing child can be obtained from the following:

*Child Find, Inc.* P.O. Box 277, New Paltz, New York 12561. Has two phone lines; one for parents wishing to list missing children (914) 255-1848; and a second, toll-free number for missing children hoping to be reunited with parents and for adults who know the whereabouts of a missing child (800) 431-4005. There is a registration fee of $60 and a preregistration option available for $10 with the purchase of a child finder kit. *Search Inc.* 560 Sylvan Avenue, Englewood Cliffs, New Jersey 07632. (201) 567-4040. Publishes a quarterly report circulated only to law enforcement agencies, medical facilities and selected social service agencies. Will advise and offer practical suggestions to parents of missing children. *National Coalition for Children's Justice:* 2998 Shelburne Road, Shelburne, Vermont 05482. (802) 985-8458. An organization, headed by Kenneth Wooden, dedicated to improving protective services for children. The coalition is working to establish a national child victim network. Will offer help with abductions by strangers, not parental snatching or runaways.

# ◼ Afterthoughts ◼

Throughout this book, I have talked about the facts involved in a variety of dangers and how to avoid them. I have stressed the importance of communicating with your child about all kinds of risks, always with the realization that it is crucial to establish family policy about safety early and clearly.

We want to do everything possible to protect our children from specific dangers and we also want to protect them from the emotional impact of these dangers. We try to be sophisticated in teaching techniques for improving their personal safety, without picturing these techniques as panaceas or turning them into obsessive rituals. Offered as common-sense approaches, lessons will be learned easily.

At the same time, I have tried to show that we can also upset and harm our children by overprotecting them, sheltering them from experiences important to their development. Children need to learn about the world and be prepared to deal with unpleasant and even painful experiences. Part of growing up is developing resources to cope with such experiences.

Nor can we, as parents, hold ourselves totally responsible for insuring a child's safety. Some factors are beyond our control—including economic realities that may not permit us to bring our children up in the safest neighborhoods. And most important, we should not let ourselves be trapped into believing that everything that happens is our fault or to our credit; that if a child comes through unscathed, it is only because we did a good job or if an unfortunate incident occurs, it means that we have been bad parents.

I hope that the guidelines offered in this book will help parents to protect their children from bad experiences and that if some incidents do happen, parents will deal with them without blaming themselves or their children. Using sound judgment, parents can do much to help their children recover from anguish or shock.

A vital step in turning concern for our children's safety into constructive action is working with the communities where we live. When people care, they pull together. Whether you live in a city or a suburb, developing an old-fashioned sense of community is the most effective antidote to crime and fear of crime.

If you are concerned about safety—or the lack of it—in your neighborhood or on your child's route to school, you can work with your local police and your child's school authorities to create a safer environment. In some instances, neighbors have joined together, with the help of the police, to form block-watch groups against crime. According to the National Sheriffs Association, the police organization which has worked toward the growth of these groups, an estimated 80,000 neighborhood block-watch groups have been formed across the country.

If you are interested in starting such a group in your area, call your local police and ask for the crime prevention section, the community relations officer or the person in charge of establishing Neighborhood Watch Programs. The information needed by the police to help you get started may vary somewhat from place to place, but general procedures for establishing a group are similar for big-city neighborhoods or small towns.

In addition, neighbors can join together to provide aid for children and be a source of help in emergencies, especially on the way to and from school. Known as Block Parent Programs, they designate a house in each neighborhood where children may seek shelter and reassurance if they are frightened, threatened or hurt. Those who volunteer to provide these "safe houses" have no legal status. They are public-spirited private citizens ready to help. Before being given a special placard to identify their homes, they are subject to a law enforcement screening. The Michigan Congress of Parents and Teachers and Students, in Lansing, adopted the Block Parent Program as far back as 1968. Many other communities in places as far apart as Utah and Alabama provide similar arrangements. For additional information call the Michigan PTA or the Utah Crime Prevention Council in Salt Lake City or the National Crime Prevention Council in Washington, D.C.

If you are a PTA member and want to establish school programs, safety assemblies are an important means of communication for students of all ages. Assemblies usually feature a local police officer trained to do such presentations. California policewoman Lori Kratzer says it is important that safety material be presented in a manner suited to each age group. When she talks to high school classes, for example, she discusses both the consequences of law breaking to the community and crime prevention techniques. With younger children, her talks are much simpler. Some suggestions for safety assemblies are offered by the New York City Parents League: Allow at least an hour; be sure to include a question period; try to create as informal a setting as possible; and limit groups to fewer than 100 students of similar ages.

Frequently, special safety programs for children are cooperative efforts, joined by several community groups. In Arizona, for example, the State Department of Public Safety, the State Superintendent of Public Instruction and the Arizona Association of Realtors joined in a statewide effort to sponsor a program called ''Safety Through Songs'' for younger children, created by Janice L. Prall in a suburb of Phoenix. In the small town of Sidney, Ohio, near Dayton, local police cooperate with the schools to offer youngsters safety programs which feature slide presentations and films.

The Crime Prevention Coalition, a national group of organizations committed to crime prevention, sponsors programs designed to stimulate everyone, parents and senior citizens as well as children, to assume responsibility for helping to prevent crime. Their material features McGruff, the floppy-eared dog in a detective's trench coat, who works to prevent crime the way that Smokey the Bear fights forest fires. If you are interested in getting their Youth Kit or other materials, contact the National Crime Prevention Council in Washington, D.C.

Seattle, Washington, is one of a number of cities where school safety instruction includes teaching children how to protect themselves from sexual molestation. Seattle's Committee for Children, a nonprofit agency, has developed an elementary school program, ''Talking about Touching: A Personal Safety

Curriculum." It is designed for kindergarten through sixth grade. "Our approach," says Committee Training Coordinator Ann Downer, "is that, just as we learn other safety rules about crossing the street and riding bikes, there are some safety rules we learn about touching."

There are programs about sexual abuse prevention in other places such as Minneapolis, Minnesota, where Cordelia Anderson Kent has created a curriculum project working out of the Hennepin County Attorney's Office.

But no matter how much help is offered by communities, it still remains a parent's duty to instruct children. We must acknowledge that our streets and our world are not as safe as we would like them to be. We must be realistic about dangers, not overplaying or underestimating them. We mislead our children if we pretend that they live in a perfect world but we also do them a disservice if we generate fear and insecurity. Our task is to show our children by example that even though crime in the streets and other dangers do exist, we are not daunted by them.

Children can learn to be wary without being fearful. They can learn that if they act sensibly, they can be as secure as it is possible to be.

Instead of being weakened by stress and adversity, families can be made stronger by facing up to reality together. Parents should view their talks with children as ways of averting excessive stress and anxiety. They can show how the family has surmounted problems. This is one of the best lessons you can teach a child.

There is a logical chain of instructions for parents to give to children. Through such safety guidance, your children will gradually gain the assurance that they have some control in coping with dangers they may face. If you move confidently in your efforts to teach your children how to protect themselves, you can take pride in success with a difficult and vital parental task.

# ▣ Index ▣

## About the Author

Grace Hechinger is a noted journalist and educator who has written extensively on family life and women's issues. She is currently a contributing columnist for *Glamour* magazine. With her husband she is the coauthor of *Teenage Tyranny*, *The New York Times Guide to New York City Private Schools*, and *Growing Up in America*. She is the mother of two sons.